GRAY POWER POLITICS

POLITICAL WANTS AND NEEDS OF THE NEWLY POWERFUL CROSS-CUTTING DEMOGRAPHIC SEGMENT

By

ROY E. PETERSON

TRICROWN BOOKS

<u>Gray Power Politics:</u>
<u>Political Wants and Needs of the Newly Powerful Cross-Cutting Segment</u>

By Roy E. Peterson

Cover Photo Credit:
Free Use of Owl Photo

Published on behalf of TriCrown Books by Kindle Direct Publishing, February 2019.

ISBN-9781793101136

Questions: <u>Kindle Publishing</u> or <u>tricrownbooks.com</u>
Available for sale on <u>amazon.com</u> and <u>Kindle.com</u>

ABOUT THE AUTHOR

Roy E. Peterson has been a master at a wide variety of occupations—a renaissance man who has won awards for his solo music abilities, ascended the officer ranks in the military, served as a Foreign Service Diplomat in Russia, was selected as the first U.S. Foreign Commercial Officer in the Russian Far East, and was a major contributor to national intelligence collection and analysis. He learned Russian, German, and Vietnamese in the military and used them in his countries of assignment. Academically, Roy E. Peterson has three Master's degrees, and over 200 postgraduate hours. He has taught for various universities in the fields of American Government, Global Business Management, American History, World History, Political Theory, and World Politics. For more see his biography at the end.

For more, see his biography at the end.

BOOKS AUTHORED BY ROY E. PETERSON

Albert: The Cat That Thought He Could Fly (Juvenile)
All American Holiday Poems (Poetry)
Alpen Splendor, Mountain Grandeur (Poetry)
American Attaché in the Moscow Maelstrom (History)
American Country Poetry: From the Prairie to the Parlor (Poetry)
American Classic Poetry: Poetry for the Majority (Poetry)
American Gold Classic Poetry: If it doesn't Rhyme…(Poetry)
American Heartland: Poetry, Wit, and Wisdom (Poetry)
American Heritage Poetry Collection (Poetry)
American Patriot Salute: Making Classic American Poems (Poetry)
Angels All Around Us: A Great Garden of Verse (Poetry)
A Pink Moon in April: Poetry from the Periphery (Poetry)
As the World Burns: Poetry by the Fireside (Poetry)
Autumn Echoes: Poetic Treasure Trove…(Poetry)
Before I Go to Bed: Rhymes for Good Times (Poetry)
Between Darkness and Light (Poetry)
Cultural Conservation Companion (Poetry)
Democratic Party Down the Rabbit Hole (Poetry)
Eternal Spring: Poetry and Promise (Poetry)
Fables from the Funny Farm (Poetry)
Feet on the Ground/Heart in the Sky (Poetry)
Fight of the Phoenix (Vietnam War Memoir and History)
For Love May Find You: Poetry with Passion (Poetry)
Grains of Sand: Poetry by the Sea (Poetry)
Guardian Angel: All My Tomorrows (Poetry)
Happy Haunting Halloween: Olde and New Classics (Poetry)
Hitler's Jewish Jet Designer (Historical Fiction)
Iron Ikon (Historical Fiction: US Foreign Service, Russia)
Love That Lasts Eternally (Poetry)
Magnetism to Marriage (Pre-Marriage Relationships)
Men and Divorce (Relationships)
Peterson Perspective (Humor, Wit, and Wisdom)
Poetry Knocking on the Door: Classic Rhymes (Poetry)
Poetry is Passion: Truth and Time in Classic Rhyme (Poetry)
Russian Romance (Historical Fiction: IBM in Russian Far East)
Soviet Intelligence Process (Out of Print Monograph)
Texas Trail Dust: Cowboy Campfire Collection (Poetry)
Where the Horny Toads Play (Life Story)
Whither My Love: Treasury of Great Classical Love Poetry (Poetry)
When I Think of Heaven (Poetry)

INTRODUCTION

Every political movement begins with a person sitting down and writing a book, writing a treatise, writing a manifesto, speaking in a Rathskeller, facing down authority that has run amuck, or starting and leading a demonstration. In the modern day, a political movement adds the power of social media to its arsenal.

I have changed the concept of the poor senior citizen, who seems inept to influence politics, bemoans the past, sits idly by on the sidelines rooting, but not too loudly, and wringing their hands in desperation at the political landscape that not only is being changed by the ignorant, the ignoble, and the incorrigible, but is impinging on our own concepts of life, liberty and happiness.

Gray Power Politics is for you, for we the people. I use "Gray Power" and "Gray "to replace the old concept of senior citizen and to incorporate an entire set of generations past the age of 50, who have tolerated too much.

To paraphrase Marx, Arise Gray Power People. You have nothing to lose, but your "pains." Get off the floor! Get involved in the political process. Do something about it. When you contact a representative or confront someone on behalf of the movement, tell them you are a member of the GPP (Gray Power Politics) movement.

I considered structuring a comprehensive organization. Heaven knows I have done that before in everything from military intelligence units to a construction company and a big security service company. Furthermore, I wrote an entire plan for a senior citizen nationwide organization about 15 years ago for a friend who was going to present it to a new organization forming in the field of senior service. I left without finding out if that is the basis for one of the organizations formed in the early 2000's. I did not ask remuneration for it. I just enjoyed the challenge.

Gray Power Politics in its nascent state of now, is an amorphous grouping that seems to have an advantage others do not. There are no dues. It is a grassroots approach to solving the problems that we have and that the nation has. If we are to have a future in common and a country that will survive the radical thunderings of the far left, then involvement must come now and not later for the salvation of us all.

You will find in the final chapter, 25 ways you can become involved in change at our age. Besides the 25 ways I give you five levels of participation in each of the 25 ways to be active. That forms a matrix of 125 actions. A few of the boxes do not quite fit, so in essence there are probably 100 ways to become involved. That is all explained for you.

During the reading I have tried to walk a middle ground between academic documentation and folksy repertoire. I feel I have accomplished this. There will be some on each side that will suggest I was either too loose with my endnotes or not stringent enough. I have interspersed personal stories through out the text that are intended to be illustrative and to bring the solutions and actions down to earth and encourage everyone in the process that I have been inordinately involved in a great many ways and will continue to be so.

Remember you have the power and my backing. The first place you could start is to purchase this book not just for yourself, but those in need of understanding what you are doing and what you expect them to do.

Roy E. Peterson
San Angelo, Texas
March 12, 2019

TABLE OF CONTENTS

Title Page   ii
About the Author   iii
Books Authored   iv
Introduction   v

1. The Gray Zone   1

2. Myths and Stereotypes   9

3. Vulnerabilities of Gray Zone Citizens   19

4. Social Security and Retirement   40

5. Health Issues and Politics   70

6. Illegal Immigration Issues Costs   100

7. Security and Self Defense   127

8. Food Safety   147

9. Changing the Political Dialogue   160

Author Biography   183

End Notes   185

Chapter 1

THE GRAY ZONE

Those over 50-years old today have the power to transform society now, since we are one of the largest cross-cutting political groups in the country. Goodness knows we have to use our remaining years to restore and insure the health of the American Republic. ~Roy E. Peterson

Who are The Gray Zone Power People?

You know them well. They are your parents and grandparents. For the lucky, they are great grandparents. They may be brothers or sisters, aunts or uncles who are single either by choice, by the death of a marriage partner, or by untimely departure of a spouse. They are you after fifty or more years of scratching out a living, saving what little and as much as you could, working hard toward a retirement that will allow you at least survival with a minimum standard of living in dignity under the social security safety net into which you have been paying hard earned wages.

They have been through foreign wars as a military veteran, spouse of a veteran, one who produced goods to win the wars, children who lost their loved ones in a war, or simply among those who also served by working in the domestic economy, planting victory gardens, or bearing children with future hopes for a better world.

They have been through depressions and recessions, banking scandals, business and personal losses, times of uncertainty as foreign threats continued to challenge their stamina and staying power, and political crises that threatened and/or changed the fabric of society, sometimes in debilitating ways.

Those who are now 80 or older were born to families during the end of the Great Depression, or even deep in the middle of it. Going even further back, some of you now 90 or more were born in the roaring 1920's.

Welcome to the Gray Zone

I am one of them. You may be one of them. We need to work together for the sake of ourselves, our family, and our society. Never underestimate the power of collaboration and teamwork. There is no ethnicity in age, although there are variants of life expectancy by ethnic group, region of the country, and farm versus urban versus city dwellers, among other differentiating factors. We are Gray Zone citizens together, to put it in a diplomatic way.

We are far from homogeneous. Our heterogeneity is reflected in the things I have just mentioned plus some additions. We are different by virtue of the usual suspects: ethnicity, gender, heritage, religion (or lack thereof), capabilities, skills, training, education, experiences, intellect, and athletic prowess. Regardless, we have a community of common interests that pulls together all these variable factors by use of "The Gray Zone." I may refer to "senior citizens," or "the elderly" on occasion although it normally will be in conjunction with a study, research, or categorization by someone else.

Now cleanse your mind of negativity. You are not a burden. I hear and read everywhere those of us in the gray zone telling everyone we do not want to be a burden on our children and/or society. Since when did we start considering that we are or would be a burden? We have worked for our children, spouses, and others. We have given of our time, skills, capabilities, intellect, and fortitude often under difficult situations and through hard times not just so we could live, but so that others could benefit. You are not a burden, and you do not get to call yourself one.

If you are American and over the age of 50, I emphasize again, count yourself in the group as being in the Gray Zone. If you are British, the spelling is "Grey." I checked book sources for any semblance of usage of either "gray" or "grey" politically with an emphasis on senior citizen involvement. I fully expected to find one with a picture of a pale gray fist either bare, or in chain mail, lifted up in significant salute or defiance. Imagine my surprise when the closest book I could find was "Fifty Shades of Grey." I have not read that book, nor do I intend to do so, but I am certain the subject matter is completely different.

I know some politically motivated enthusiast out there is going to challenge why I start the Gray Zone at the age of 50, when most senior citizen studies of the aging begin at the age of 65. Most retirement communities in states such as California have the provision that the purchaser must be 55-years of age.

1. I began with the concept that those who reach the "round birthday" age of 50 suddenly look ahead to retirement and what awaits them in the future. There have been studies of when a person begins to recognize the need for retirement savings, planning for where to go or whether to stay to live out life, thoughts about downsizing and changing priorities, and paying more attention to things that affect older citizens. That is at the age of 50, although most still will assert they are middle aged.

2. A second reason is the two largest advocacy/lobbying organizations, and service providers for senior citizens have become increasingly responsive not just to the retired set, but those who reach the age of 50 in allowing membership. The

Association of Mature American Citizens (AMAC) uses the slogan, "The Voice of Americans 50+" AARP (now just using the initials, but formerly The American Association of Retired Persons) has shifted its focus onto those who become 50 years of age, as well. For your information AARP jettisoned the original name in 1999. I presume the reason was to expand the membership range for the audience and services they provide, shifting from the retired stigma.

3. I like the terms "Gray Power "and "Gray Zone," because it expunges some of the pejorative connotation that has become associated with senior citizens, openly embraces those whose focuses are shifting gears, and provides an identification factor with the entire range of the demographic.

As a political scientist, my purpose is to remain objective in my approach and rely on the presentation of empirical evidence, data, and statistical analysis. I am aided and abetted by always being a pragmatic moderate in politics, choosing to vote on the issues, not the politician's appearance or facile tongue, nor on the political party with which he or she is branded.

Fortunately, those of us over fifty are not the only ones interested in the gray political cross-cutting segment of voters, spenders, thought shapers, or any other social activists. Everyone should read and pay attention to the logical arguments I am presenting and the information contained in this book. After all, I will be laying out their own future prospects, or lack thereof.

Actuarial Table of Live Expectancy

Those who speak of sixty being the new fifty are partially correct. Based on life expectancy rates past as projected in 1950, US women could expect to live to the age of 71, men to the age of 65, for a combined total average of 68 years. Those figures have increased by 11 years to the age of

79+ for the projected combined actuarial death table column of 2020, as well as for both men and women.

Table 1-1: Actuarial Table[1]

Year	Women	Men	Combined
1950	71.10	65.60	68.20
1960	73.10	66.60	69.70
1970	74.30	67.10	70.80
1980	77.40	70.00	73.70
1991	78.90	72.00	75.50
2000	79.49	73.90	76.62
2010	81.45	75.55	78.42
2020	82.93	76.85	79.82

Note: No Data for 1990. Source: Data 360:
http://data360.org/dsg.aspx?Data_Set_Group_Id=195

There are other statistical tables including ones from the distant past where the entire year has become deceased, but that is of little use to us in the present. We would have to go back more than 100 years for that information.

We are thrust together in the same leaky boat dependent upon the political ocean and its waves tossing us about. We need to seize the oars and all begin rowing in the same direction. We have that capability, yet we have deferred to younger generations and unsound practices foisted upon us by our own generations leaving us frustrated and without a compass.

There are some factors that impact the overall demographic pattern such as foreign-born population. In 1965, foreign born population was just 5% of the population. Nearly 39 million legal immigrants entered the country since then for a total of 14% of the US population in 2015. That number is rapidly increasing in 2019, since February had 75,000 and March is headed for 100,000 with new caravans planning an invasion. That has major significance such as how much money will be absorbed to pay continuing welfare, how many of them will find an illegal way to retire under our Social Security System. When are we going to seal our system to benefit only our own citizens and stop expanding programs?

According to the U.S. Census Bureau Quick Facts, the population of the United States was just over 308,000,000 in 2010. The U.S. Census Bureau estimated the U.S. population as of July 1, 2018 at 327,719,178. The next census is scheduled for the normal sequencing in 2020 and is expected to show over 330,000,000. From the estimate base of 2010, those age 65 or older compose 15.6% of the population. The total number estimated over 65 reached 50 million for the first time in 2014.[2] With the group aged 50 to 64 added into the equation, those I place in the Gray Zone represent 30% of the population and their tendency to vote is much higher at around 40% of total voters. That is the political power of Gray!

Imagine what we can accomplish with 40% of the vote. Furthermore, that number continues to grow, since by all government demographic accounts the population of the United States continues to rise including not only past 50, but past the age of 65. Within 10 years those age 65 and older will reach 20% giving at least an additional 10% boost to those who vote. As you know those under age 18 cannot vote and that is a significant percentage that is set aside, though I heard on the news today that in Massachusetts they are considering a bill to reduce the age to 16. Now what 16-year old had lived long enough to understand political phenomena. In many high schools they do not even teach civics anymore. Obviously, the political party in power in that state at the time (March 10, 2019) believes they will get an additional advantage in the vote. Regardless, the Gray Power Politics population can approach a majority on the voting roles.)

You may have noted I do not use supposedly politically correct words. If you need that go somewhere else. The population has not yet added a third category for gender as of this writing, although I have heard some rumblings about forcing the U.S. Census Bureau to add such a category to the 2020 Census. I refuse to use the category and it is not important to this discussion anyway, since age does not respect sex either, except for what happens and to whom, health wise or otherwise. We can add age, ethnicity, natural born American and other categories in later discussions such as health issues, but for now I am talking about the entire age category having political clout!

Fix the Problem or it Fixes You

Somewhere along the way I learned this headline both as a saying and a practical life situation that came back to bite me. In fixing problems there are various ways, approaches, and methods to solve it. The first decision point for me is to use my knowledge, experience and logic to ascertain if it is important to do one of the following: a.) Work toward a solution, or b.) Pass the problem off to someone else, or c.) Ignore the problem, or d.) Postpone the resolution in the hopes it will either pass or solve itself, or e.) Kill it!

If you look at a five, six, or seven step approach to take on a problem as presented in some literature, the first step always is to define the problem. Defining and redefining is actually a creative step, since it helps establish the scope of the problem and point the way toward alternative solutions. I recognize that defining the problem is often the most difficult task including is it a problem in the first place for us. Key variables that go into the definitions, especially for societal, political and economic problems is the priorities in our minds set by a.) Religion, b.) Culture, c.) Upbringing, d.) Acquired Knowledge, and e.) Experience.

The reason I hedged on the number of steps is some problems require relatively simple solutions that do not involve research and information collection, but others do. I use a nine-step approach for complex problems and place a time on the final date for resolution. Let me delineate my own process:

Peterson Preferred Nine-Step Model of Problem Solving

Why would I present my nine-step model of problem solving? First, because I have seen five to seven step ones and I believed they needed a couple more steps. Second, because it is how I tend to approach writing and information presentation: 1.) Definition—2.) Analysis—3.) Information Collection—4.) Revise Analysis—5.) Alternative Solutions—6.) Solutions Testing—7.) Solution Selection—8.) Plan of Action—9.) Implement.

The next few chapters will deal with the problems faced by the Gray Zone, some as a result of the vulnerabilities in this chapter, some caused by groups and organizations, and some caused by the government. I will be thinking of this process in my presentation of materials. I will always provide my "preferred solution" based on critical thinking in my nine-step model. You may accept it or come up with something better or worse, but at least you will have a thought base to accept or deviate. I am asking you to set aside your fifty years involvement in the processes and concentrate on what you find is the best thing for you as a Gray Zone partner and for future Americans. I suspect deviations will be only minor and we can push ahead for reforms at every level to secure not only what we want, but what we need. Most of all we want what is best for our country.

Chapter 2

MYTHS AND STEREOTYPES

More than half the people who ever lived to be 65 are alive today. ~Jeanne Sather

A long time ago I had a friend who told me, "I love older people. I want to be one someday." That thought stuck with me. I read a research report one time that showed elderly people do not innately smell bad. Young people and old people were in the study. They all took a shower using neutral unscented soap. Then they put on clothes washed in the same washer with the same unscented soap. Sniffers were blindfolded and asked if they could tell the difference in young and elderly people, men or women, and ethnicity. The results of the survey were everyone smelled the same.

If we think the elderly smell bad automatically, then we are wrong and already biased on that one point alone. Hygiene is the key. If we become lackadaisical about hygiene, of course then we smell bad to others. The thought applies politically. If we simply attempt to dismiss something politically without an explanation, then we stink in that sense too. We need to exercise our minds and explain situations, use our intelligence and logic, provide our experiences and demonstrate from history our views.

Just as there is the myth that older people smell bad, there are a lot of myths that are in the minds of the younger generation. These myths are often propagated by senior citizens themselves making jokes, a popular culture that has not been taught properly to respect their elders, news media that emphasizes sensationalism, and salacious social media that perpetuates "funny" graphics and memes.

I recently read an article from <u>Senior Planet</u> in which seven myths about older people were briefly discussed. I combined that with my own research to come up with additional myths. Then I add two more myths about the Gray Zone population and firearms.

Myth #1: So Many Senior Citizens have Alzheimer's their Cognition is Suspect

Reality: Those with Alzheimer's constitute only 2.6 to 5.1 million.[1] The US Population over 65 in 2016 was 46 million.[2] 27 million Americans (10% of the US Population over 12) reported using illicit drugs in 2014 and 28.7 million (10.8% of US population over 12) drove intoxicated at least once in 2013.[3] Our Gray Zone is far more capable to make reasonable and valid political decisions.

Table 2-1: Alzheimer's vs Abusers

Alzheimer's	2.6 million
Drugs/Alcohol	55.7 million

Myth #2: Senior citizens mostly live in nursing homes.

Reality: According to the U.S. Bureau of the Census, only 5% over 65 live in nursing homes.[4] According to AARP, "only 2% of Americans age 65 to 84 and 14% age 85 or older live in nursing homes."[5]

Myth #3: Aging dulls communication abilities.

Reality: Older people have greater communication abilities based on language usage and experience than presumed. "While seniors may have slower reaction times, 'mental capabilities that depend most heavily on accumulated experience and knowledge, like settling disputes and enlarging one's vocabulary, clearly get better over time,' writes Patricia Cohen in the <u>New York Times</u>."[7]

Myth #4: Senior citizens are not active. They mostly vegetate all day and sometimes at night.

Reality: Who do you think crowds the cruise ship lines? Who travels everywhere? Who do you see most in Walmart? The last one may be a given, since Walmart fills millions of prescriptions, but senior citizens are more than sedentary. This is a stereotype. I read in one blog that a senior strength and fitness personal coach may become a "trending career."[8]

Myth #5: Senior Citizens have the most vehicle accidents of any class of driver.

Reality: "The FACTS" according to the <u>Statistical Abstract of the United States</u> (2010) are these:

Table 2-2: Driver Age and Accidents

Driver Age	Number of Drivers	Accidents
65+	30,567,000	1,350,000
16-20	12,906,000	2,770,000

Seniors have almost $2^{1/2}$ times the number of drivers and half the accidents! That makes the likelihood of a teen causing an accident almost 5 times as much as a senior citizen.[9]

Myth #6: Senior citizens cannot be interested in sex, or at least have a lower libido.

Reality: Have you not heard about the "dirty old man" jokes? Joan Price is a sexpert who has written books like "Naked at Our Age" and "The Ultimate Guide to Sex Over 50." Isabelle Kohn in an article in Harpers Bazaar (October 2018) wrote, "Not only is senior sex better than younger sex, reveals sex expert Joan Price, but millennials could actually master a more fulfilling iteration of lovemaking from their elders — one that's based on extended arousal and less pressure to perform."[10] Perhaps it has always been this way as far as fulfilling; however, it is reasonable to assume these days that a boost from a "little blue pill" adds a lot to performance.

Myth #7: Aging makes a person less creative.

Reality: In fact, the opposite is true for a great many people who could have been creative at any age, except for various reasons such as raising families, or struggling with careers while raising money to support their families.

The foremost example is that of Grandma Moses, who did not start painting until the age of 80, but basically was the founder, or at least foremost practitioner of the naïve art movement. She painted until the age of 100.

At one time I was going to write a book about successful people who did not begin until late in life. Julia Child was not known until she was in her 50's.

Colonel Sanders was a relatively impoverished restaurant chef until he worked out his discovered secret spice recipe of 11 herbs and spices by experimentation at the age of 65.

The first successful book of Frank McCourt, "Angela's Ashes," started his career as a late bloomer at the age of 66.

Laura Ingalls Wilder did not get her first book, "Little House on the Big Prairie," published until the age of 66 and was still writing when she died at age 90.

Winston Churchill was a pariah just before World War II and then at the age of 65 replaced Neville Chamberlain as

Prime Minister, serving off and on to the age of 80.

: Aging is depressing to senior adults.

Table 2-3: Age and Happiness[10a]

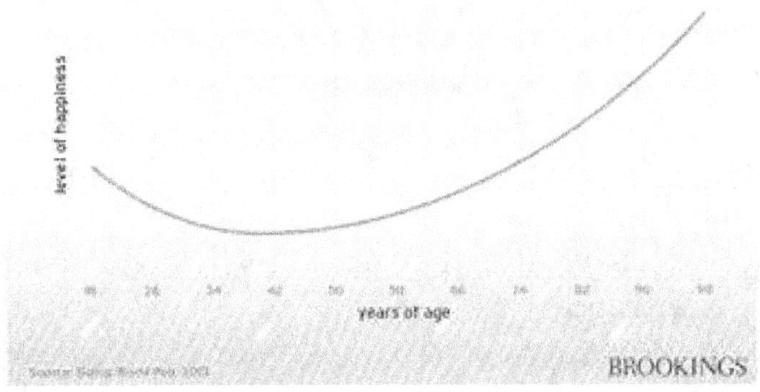

Reality: Contrary to the myths and stereotypes, senior adults are the happiest. As one author points out, the charted curve for happiness is a U-shape with senior adults in the United States the happiest.[11]

Myth #9: Senior citizens cannot learn new skills.

Reality: As it turns out, senior citizens can learn new skills if they have a desire to do so. Adaptability, creativity, and learning are not exclusive to the young or middle aged. There may be some cognitive slowing, but learning continues throughout life unless one suffers a stroke, suffers from Alzheimer's, or gets a serious impairment like loss of hearing or blindness. Even in those cases, seniors are adaptable and capable of learning through their new filters.[12]

Myth #10: Aging makes a person unproductive.

Reality: Retirement does not mean becoming unproductive. Child-rearing in place of working parents, volunteering, finding new jobs and engaging in hobbies can all have a great impact of society and the personal lives of friends and relatives. The Bureau of Labor Statistics shows 24% of senior citizens engage in volunteer work, for example.[13]

Myth #11: Aging makes a person more religious.

Reality: Aging has only a limited effect on religious views. To be sure those views may become more pronounced to others, especially since they have less to lose, like a job, but church attendance, for example, is a "generational phenomenon rather than an aging phenomenon… Today's seniors haven't become more religious with time. Instead, they grew up in a time when more people went to church, which is why seniors are the most religious age group."[11]

Myth #12: Senior citizens have a greater fear of death.

Reality: According to the National Institute on Aging, most older people are not obsessed with death or dying.[14]

Myths persist as a way for a people or culture to make sense out of their world. Over time they become stereotypes that are not based on reality, but come from a myth or series of myths.[15] Stereotypes can be prejudicial and dangerous when dealing with gender, race, religion, and age. Some of them have persisted so long it is like they became gospel.

Everything about senior citizens, though has been changing with the medications and innovations of science that have extend our average living time by 12 more years in the past few decades. I saw an interesting statement: Half of all the people ever to reach the age of 65 are living now![16] Writing on myths of the aging, Jeanne Sather, wrote "That alone suggests that myths about again based on past generations may not hold true for this one."[16]

The twelve myths I listed are the major ones I selected from different sources after conducting research, but there are so many more out there. NPO provided a list of some of the most frequently heard myths from research by the MacArthur Foundation:

> #1: To be old is to be sick.
> #2: You can't teach an old dog new tricks.
> #3: The horse is out of the barn.
> #4: The secret to successful aging is to choose
>   your parents wisely.
> #5: The lights may be on, but the voltage is low.
> #6: The elderly don't pull their own weight.[14]

Would our contemporary society permit these myths to be bandied about if they related to gender, ethnic group, religious group, country of origin, or any other category? You may answer yes or no, but the fact is they are constantly in the media and in social communication, cartoons and verbal speech without apology. I exploded the twelve myths with research and logic.

The point I wish to make in this book is that the Gray Zone citizens are fully capable of defending themselves and becoming political power segment, even more so than other cross-cutting segments of society.

There are two more myths that have a major impact on senior citizens, or if not yet, certainly will with bad legislation being proposed all the time to control "guns."

There are two myths about senior citizens and guns that are propagated by the anti-gun left as they continually attempt to subvert the U.S. Constitution and the Bill of Rights.

Myth 1: Senior citizens rarely must confront a threat requiring a weapon.[17] Wrong!

Reality: A. Threats to senior citizens are more common than most imagine. There is a column in the regular NRA publications titled, "The Armed Citizen."[17] In this regular column, attacks on senior citizens are detailed with them successfully defending themselves with firearms around the whole country. That goes for both men and women.

B. Most fail to realize that a burglar facing a weapon will likely be surprised and deterred at the same time. The burglar may surrender, or the person sometimes releases them with a warning. Some of the cases are never reported to police and some sources do not have the age of the intended victim.

C. As so many of my Texas friends have pointed out, the difference in reaction time is now versus at least a 15-minute response time assuming the senior citizen can even gain access to a telephone. By the way, not being able to get to a telephone, because the threat is between the intended victim and the phone is something rarely mentioned but has a high probability in real-life experience. Just ask the police.

D. In any event, the most likely outcome is not a shooting by either the threat or the potential victim when the potential victim has a firearm in his or her hands.

E. Predators believe senior citizens are easy targets until confronted with a firearm. Not only is a firearm the best defense, it may be the only defense.

Myth 2: Firearms are not an advantage for senior citizens in a criminal attack.

Reality: Now I know someone's brains are filled with marshmallow fluff. As the writer of the NRA article I used for this source said, criminals think senior citizens cannot use firearms effectively, and so they will simply attack and severely injure them or shoot them with theirs or the owner's gun. He answered his own question: "What else besides a firearm gives an elderly person any kind of a fair chance against a younger, more physically powerful aggressor?"

I have to laugh, since I cannot understand the thinking process. If a senior citizen has a gun, he likely has had excellent training in its use in the military, in hunting, or in target practice. Besides a half blind person can shoot a squirrel at ten paces.

The Gray Zone Citizens Must Unite for Action

I have never been one to celebrate diversity in American culture other than to enjoy some of the food and customs they retained. I choose to celebrate unity, especially unity of action to satisfy our wants and needs both materially and politically. We have the power. We just have to realize it and press forward together in a concerted effort to change not just attitudes, but laws and decision making in our state government and in our national Congress while altering and shaping public policy and benefits that affect us.

I conclude this chapter with the conclusions of Dr. John Rowe and Dr. Robert Kahn as quoted in NPO, "...our society is in persistent denial of some important truths about aging. Our perceptions about the elderly fail to keep pace with the dramatic changes in their actual status. We view the aged as sick, demented, frail, weak, disabled, powerless, sexless, passive, alone, unhappy, and unable to learn — in short, a rapidly growing mass of irreversibly ill, irretrievable older Americans. To sum up, the elderly are depicted as a figurative ball-and-chain holding back an otherwise spry collective society."[19]

I have news for millennials! The Gray Zone is growing larger every year and expected to double again by the year 2060. In the meantime, the younger generations are shrinking with spectacular abortion numbers and drug abuse deaths among other things. Guess who is going to rule the country in the near future, not just by the elderly, but for the elderly.

I despise the term political correctness, since it impinges on free speech. I found though that changing terms in a discussion changes the outcomes of debate. With that in mind social scientists and "other enlightened professionals are taking a leading role in creating and introducing new metaphors intended to cast a motivating optimistic aura about again.'"[18]

We simply have to unify in expressing our needs and wants politically through contact, writing, press releases, public appearances, demonstrations, blogs and any other means of social action. The Medicare system is once again up for revision and Social Security decisions will impact our age group until we put a stop to what is going on and demand change that is positive for the Gray Zone. What is positive for the Gray Zone is positive for society!

Chapter 3

VULNERABILITIES OF GRAY ZONE CITIZENS

Senior Citizens fear losing their independence more than they fear Death. ~ "Aging in Place in America," Prince Market Research, 2007.

Since I am a member of the Gray Zone, I will share some personal experiences as well as information and data from trusted sources. Gray Zone vulnerabilities are similar to vulnerabilities for the general population; however, they are more impactful, since they drain critical retirement resources, there are fewer or no work years to replace what has been lost or stolen, and they are particularly psychologically harmful leading to depression, withdrawal, fears, and insecurity.

A personal story. I did some research on communications packages from various vendors involving television, phone and internet. I felt I did some good comparative research online to bring my package of service down from $183 per month. My cable package that I left-did not include any premium channel, or the cost would have been over $200 monthly (at least $2,400 per annum). Just to give you a hint, the $183 per month was approximately 5% of my annual retirement income including Social Security. I was able to "cut the cable" portion dramatically, while keeping the phone and high-speed internet. I was about to change to another provider for phone and internet, but discovered the internet speed would drop from 50 megabytes (mbps) per second to 3 mbps. That meant more than half the time a video would be stalling and buffering.

I had placed the order, but kept checking and

discovered the difference. I do not claim technological sophistication, but I do understand that difference. The problem was in talking with the representative of the new company I was not told, or did not hear the vast difference in speed. I did not need it for games, but I certainly needed it for things like music videos and social media. I was able to overcome my vulnerability and cancel the phone/internet installation switch, but wonder how many others are stuck with a bad system at least for a contract of one year in duration.

Forget whether you have historically voted Democrat or Republican. When you reach the Gray Zone, and even before you should be committed to what the future Congressional Senators and Representatives will do or not do for the aging population, while still securing the benefits of the Republic for our children and grandchildren. I may have an advantage here because my father always tended to vote Democrat and my mother voted Republican on the issues over the span of their lives. I often said I came from a split family, but it was divided only politically.

Changes to the Economy

The economy is constantly changing, but changes in tax structure, raises in minimum wages, governmental waste on social programs, and inflation all conspire to damage those in the gray zone the most. Mark Twain certainly had the most memorable quote that I remembered that lumped together the political and economic dimensions of government: "No man's life, liberty, or property are safe while the Congress is in session." This was amplified by President Woodrow Wilson, how said: "Liberty has never come from the government; it has always come from the subjects of it. The history of liberty is a history of limitation of governmental power, not the increase of it." While you puzzle over why such overtly political quotes appear here, I will tell you they are symptomatic of the governmental decisions affecting our economic wellbeing.

Federal, state, county and local jurisdictions all have shifting tax rates covering income, personal property, sales, and special purpose taxes. These changes usually increase over time despite short periods of attempts to lower some of them as under the present administration. Various political jurisdictions often do have discounts or exemptions for various categories such as a portion of federal tax for Social Security payees, Veterans, Railroad Commissions and Railroad Retirement. I will specifically take on the Social Security taxes and the legally passed, but onerous payments that are really taxes in the form of Medicare/Medicaid deductions. I will slam these in the Retirement/Social Security chapter.

The minimum wage debate never seems to consider that raising it by government passage of a law is a Socialist measure that intervenes in the free market to the detriment of retirees and any with fixed incomes. In recent years states such as California, New York, and New Jersey have steps in place to reach $15 per hour minimum wage by 2020 to 2022. Some cities have already implemented laws sending wages to $15 per hour including Seattle, Los Angeles, San Francisco, and Chicago. So far, the studies are I found discuss the highly negative effect on the wage earners themselves without taking into account the gray zone ones with fixed wages over the age of 65, who now finding eating out a luxury they can no longer afford.

I take some satisfaction that the majority of studies, though a small sample to be sure demonstrate that wage earners earn less per month with higher wages as employers take steps to limit the labor cost of their franchises and stores. They mostly examined the fast food and restaurant industries so far. Here are the results:

1. California: "The statewide minimum wage in California gradually rose from $6.75 in 2006 to $10.50 in 2017, and it is slated to hit $15 in 2022. A team of economists at the University of California-Los Angeles examined the effect of the hikes so far, focusing on the impact on the restaurant industry. Here's what they estimate: 'the increments in the minimum wage from 6.75 to $7.50 in 2007 and to $8 in 2008 were estimated to increase earnings in limited service restaurants slightly more than 10%, but reduced employment by another 10 percent."[3]

2. Seattle: "Economists from the University of Washington presented a paper on the effects of the minimum wage in Seattle, which is headed toward $15 for all employers by 2021. That paper…found that on average the minimum wage increases have cause employers to reduce hours, with a net effect of reducing low-wage employees' earnings by $125 month. Wonkblog noted…the paper's conclusions…have left many researchers scratching their heads."[4]

3. Chicago: Found "minor" losses.[5]

Why did I include these conclusions when clearly it is talking about just the effects of government intervention in the free market workplace? Two reasons: a.) If they kept the same level of employment, the Gray Zone fixed income population could ill-afford even a Friday night fast food restaurant outing and b.) Gray Zone workers who have tried to find temporary work in such an industry are further limited.

Any change to the economy that mandatorily increases costs simultaneously is an affront, an insult, and hurts Gray Zone populations disproportionately. We can do something about this at the ballot box, but we have to make sure the candidates we select to run as our representatives at all levels have not only our input, but our oversight. We have to challenge all participants and all political parties to do the right thing for the Gray Zone. In fact, we deserve it and we demand it!

Crime

Who does not worry about crime? Well, I suppose I could answer the criminals, even the retired ones, but for the Gray Zone, crime is always at or close to the top of issues to be addressed. If there is a way to prevent even one crime, would you put measures in place to save that one person? How many crimes involving homicide, theft, violence, assault, and rape does it take to get our communities, states, and nation aroused enough to do something about it?

The first step in crime prevention is to keep people out—out of the house, out of the town, out of the state, and out of the country. My focus is on the pressure the Gray Zone can put on legislators to prevent criminals from coming to this country. That means, gasp, yes, border security! If even one American is killed by not having preventive measures from getting to the United States, that is too high a price to pay. I have found it hard to believe, but have to accept that some criminals have invaded our country as many as seven times and killed more than one person during their illegal time here! Common and sense and logic says that only by legal entry that includes criminal background checks among other civilized acceptance measures (no disease, no habitually indigent, etc.) can we at least have a reasonable expectation that the immigrant will have prospects of being a productive U.S. citizen and have a reasonable belief they will not commit a crime and certainly not a homicide.

Consider the crime statistics of illegal aliens that are disproportionately high to the overall American population! I will present two initial sets of data (call them facts if you want) on illegal aliens and crime. The Department of Justice in 2015 said that "illegals are 3.5% of the population of the USA, but they commit: 12 % of the murders, 20% of kidnappings, 16% of drug trafficking.[6] Meanwhile in Texas illegals commit 20.42% of the murders, 15.78% of sexual assaults, 14.7% of the burglaries, and 9.5% of assaults.[7]

We know there are ways to prevent and stop crimes by illegal aliens in the first place. That is to keep them out of our backyard! So why are measures proposed and not taken? What is wrong with our society, with our representatives, with Congress? The answer is ballot box accountability. Did we forget how to use it and allow crime to happen? More on this subject in another chapter.

Fraud and Scams

There are several reasons for targeting the Gray Zone depending on the nature of the scam. From research and my own inclinations, those of us who have reached this age are relatively unsophisticated in computer or mobile phone technology. We often have password problems. We have a kindness for others and a fondness for certain things like children. We would love to augment our income on a quick fix approach, protect ourselves from identity theft, secure our financial resources, and pay less for things. Scammers consider any and all of those wishes in constructing their approaches.

While conducting research, I decided to highlight the eleven most pervasive types of fraud, scams, and schemes against those of us in the Gray Zone. All of these are also used on the general population; however, like so many things Gray Zone people are the most affected, generally the least able to recover from the scam, and the most susceptible. As the National Council of Aging wrote, "Financial scams targeting seniors have become so prevalent that they're now considered 'the crime of the 21st Century.'"[8]

1. Counterfeit Prescription Drugs: Do I need to highlight the dangers of counterfeit drugs? I can begin with out of date drugs found in a landfill, pure placebo pills that have no medical value, pills that have various dangerous substances in them as cheap replacements for the costlier medications, and pills produced in foreign facilities without quality controls, or in-home labs! The cost is not only the price, but what such pills may or may not do to the system of the purchaser. I would never buy a medication touted as coming from Canada and being cheaper, since it may have been made there, or not! It could have been made in Bangladesh for all I know. Peter J. Pitts published an article in The <u>Washington Times</u> that mentioned only the tip of the iceberg:

"Importing drugs from **Canada** is exceedingly dangerous for a number of reasons.....The EU currently operates under a system of "parallel trade," which allows products to be freely imported between member countries. This means that any drugs exported from the United Kingdom to Canada that could have originated in an EU country with significantly less rigorous safety regulations, like Greece, Portugal, Latvia or Malta.

Just last year, EU officials seized more than 34 million fake pills in just two months. And in May, Irish drug enforcers confiscated over 1.7 million pounds of counterfeit and illegal drug packages. So, if American customers start buying drugs over the internet from Canadian pharmacies, they could easily wind up with tainted medicines of unknown European origin."[9]

2. Door Knockers: Have you had door knockers recently that want you to try a sketchy green liquid product touted to clean everything? I did in late January 2019. The label supposedly had eco-friendly chemicals, but it looked homemade to me. It could have been hydrochloric acid that certainly would have not only cleaned, but eaten into every surface it contacted from countertops to toilet bowls.

I was then reminded of when I grew up on a farm in South Dakota and the Gypsies, as they were called then and likely were, came to our farm eight miles out of town with a hard luck story and said they had to have money. My mother and I were the only ones around the house and were approached by a lady in our garden. She appeared out of nowhere and started telling a sob story. My mother, who often gave even from our meager income at the time for charitable causes, stopped her immediately and told her to leave. I was about ten years old. The lady at first refused to retreat until I raised my hoe. Then she hastened down the lane to a better car than we had out on the main road. My mother then instructed me that if no one were home, they might have stolen what they could. She said, "Think for yourself. Why are they way out here in the country asking at a farm house? They will hit each farm and then speed away." Sure enough, that Saturday night when all the farm families came to town, the discussion was about the Gypsies and worries that they might still be around. Every farm family had been approached. Common sense told me as a young boy (with the assistance of my mother) that if they were really desperate, they would have gone into town and not have gone out to the farms. Sure enough, they had also hit our small town of about 500 people, but then they went to the farms.

There was a hard luck story associated with the green chemical product presented the other day. In fact, this was the third time someone came to the door with a similar product in the past couple of years. In two cases they stated they were reformed criminals restarting their lives by honorably selling something useful. What really turned me off was when they said they would be glad to come inside to show me how it worked. That threw my guard up another notch. One of them told me the bottle cost $30, since it worked so well. Guess what? Hydrogen Peroxide, Vinegar, Scrubbing Bubbles, Clorox products, and Lime-away cost at least three times less! They are all under $10 with hydrogen peroxide less than $1 a bottle.

3. Fraudulent Anti-aging Products: As a male member of the species, I am not particularly into anti-aging products, not even hair restoration. I have enough. I don't think I have met a woman yet who does not want to look younger. Anti-aging sales pitches take advantage of this trait suffusing us with ads including creams, ointments, and of course, Botox. Beware. As the NCOA points out, "It is in this spirit that many older Americans seek out new treatments and medications to maintain a youthful appearance, putting them at risk of scammers. Whether it's fake Botox like the one in Arizona that netted its distributors (who were convicted and jailed in 2006) $1.5 million in barely a year, or completely bogus homeopathic remedies that do absolutely nothing, there is money in the anti-aging business.

Botox scams are particularly unsettling, as renegade labs creating versions of the real thing may still be working with the root ingredient, botulism neurotoxin, which is one of the most toxic substances known to science. A bad batch can have health consequences far beyond wrinkles or drooping neck muscles."[8]

4. Funeral and Cemetery Scams: The FBI has warnings of funeral and cemetery expenses in which the grieving are conned out of extra payments, such as in a cremation which should cost $600, or less, but which may have an added casket charge of thousands of dollars or some other cost not associated with cremation, Cremation is done using a cardboard box! I still think $600 is too much. Even funeral homes that are established a long time in a hometown, may be significantly overcharging. Question all costs. In the second related scam there actually are grifters who appear at funerals. "In one approach, scammers read obituaries and call or attend the funeral service of a complete stranger to take advantage of the grieving widow or widower. Claiming the deceased had an outstanding debt with them, scammers will try to extort money from relatives to settle the fake debts."[8]

5. Homeowner/Reverse Mortgage Scams: The likelihood of those who are in the Gray Zone and retired having extensive equity in their home is high. I would say almost a certainty unless they rented all their life. That makes them a prime target for homeowner and reverse mortgage scams. Now I do not think that Tom Selleck, who I have seen recently on TV ads for reverse mortgage companies, is touting a scam, but even there you better pay close attention as to what they are doing with you house and who keeps the deed and then who inherits the place after departure.

NCOA warns, "Those considering reverse mortgages should be cognizant of people in their lives pressuring them to obtain a reverse mortgage, or those that stand to benefit from the borrower accessing equity, such as home repair companies who approach the older adult directly."[8]

Beware of anyone offering to arrange a reassessment of your property value with the county assessor saying you should have less of a tax burden. Of course, they will charge a fee for a simple process you could perform yourself.

6. Identity Theft: I believe there are not many of us who have never heard of identity theft for voting fraud, social security fraud, and bank fraud. Identify theft has become extremely prevalent in recent years and as always, the victims who can least afford to lose money are those in the Gray Zone. LifeLock and other companies promise complete protection and recovery/repayment of funds. Banks finally have adopted measures such as putting stops on questionable transactions, limiting the damage, and taking it on themselves to pursue the scammers. In the meantime, you have problems that could include damaged credit scores and empty bank accounts.

7. Internet Fraud: Older individuals likely are the easiest targets for Internet scams. They are a ubiquitous fact of life on emails, in viruses used for blackmail, and on social media accounts. "Pop-up browser windows simulating virus-scanning software will fool victims into either downloading a fake anti-virus program (at a substantial cost) or an actual virus that will open up whatever information is on the user's computer to scammers…unfamiliarity with the less visible aspects of browsing the web (firewalls and built-in virus protection, for example) make seniors especially susceptible to such traps."[8]

Personal story. While writing this I checked my email. There was a notification of $11 on hold with PayPal. Next to it was a link that presumably would have taken me directly there to dispute the transaction, knowing that it was small, and they were trying to protect me. Of course, I had to enter my login coordinates and did so. Immediately a screen popped up with a yellow background requiring full input of everything from social security number to accounts. Then it struck me I was about to be the victim of a major scam using PayPal as a false front. I immediately jumped out of the email, logged in to PayPal and changed my password. I realized I was fortunate, because often these scammers will quickly pickup on the password you gave them and change it so only they have access to your account.

The email scams that are phishing scams always ask you, either, or verify your account using personal information such as social security number. Doing so mean you are not only falling victim to this one time shot, but to a wide range of scams as they either use for themselves or sell you information on the dark web. I have received email scams from everything included in the telephone scams you will read about in #10 below to IRS statements about a tax refund you are due.

A second personal story. (BA Scam and account freeze.)

8. Investment Schemes: Thanks to television shows like "American Greed," we have become more educated about pyramid schemes, Ponzi schemes, high return on risk free investments, and affinity fraud.

Daniel Krueger in his book, "The Secret Language of Money,"[10] lists seven types of financial scams. His book sums up the greatest number of financial scams. He gives an excellent list that is certainly instructive, but there are more like the manager of a trust fund skimming or embezzling funds; buying something at a yard sale that the purchaser recognizes as of high value, but it is sold for next to nothing; and appraisals of antiques or other high value items at a low price and then trying to buy them for that amount. Anyway, here is a discussion of the seven included in Krueger's book:

"Soft Scams: A product or company is real, but the con artists misrepresent the product to make it seem so much more valuable, and then offers you a chance to invest. This also applies to unscrupulous Stock Brokers, and Money Managers.

Hard Scams: Nonexistent products and companies are used to attract and recruit potential investors, and are promised a premium for recruiting others.

Bad Investments: A high rate of return like 10% to 20%, or sometimes an insane return on money is promised for investment in a product or company that does not exist.

Affinity Scams: The con artist takes advantage of a group to which the victim belongs. These are easy to categorize such as ethnic groups, religious groups, professional groups, and any group that is readily identifiable.

The scammer may be a member of the group, or pretend to be a member of the group they are using as the host for the scam. They may even have promised some small return to a leader in the group and pay them off as the go, such as 10% on every transaction they bring to the scam.

Identity Theft: The scam is...used for investment purposes with someone passing themselves off as President of a company, complete with certificates on the wall no less, or a Wharton Business Scholl Certificate framed behind a massive antique beautiful desk. Office space may be rented for only a short time and the con artist(s) can disappear in a moment's notice and move to another city and state.

Internet Investment: (These) are hackers who acquire personal information and passwords, make fraudulent loan offers, or sell something on a fake website.

Pyramid schemes often referred to Ponzi Schemes after the great con artist of a century ago. Probably the scheme that got the most press attention in recent times was the massive Bernie Madoff investment fraud. Pyramid and Ponzi schemes count on their survival by continuously bringing in new money with victims that assist in paying the guaranteed high return on the investment of others. At some point, of course, the whole scheme falls like a house of cards."[10]

I have always been amazed by these schemes, since the perpetrators almost never invest the money that actually could have been used to acquire substantial goods and products. They could have lived as high off the hog, kept half the investors' money and used the income from the portion of money they did invest to eventually repay every investor.

9. Medicare/Health Insurance Scams: This would seem to be difficult on the face of it with government checks on payments; however, just think of all the people charged with fraud over recent years at legitimate places, let alone sleaze-bags. I have a constant barrage of phone calls for medical alert bracelets, supposedly helpful people wanting to make sure I get all to which I am entitled by giving them my information, and products that they are certain I can claim for Medicare repayment if I only purchase them. One repetitive product is back braces! Some may be legitimate, but why take the chance.

According to the National Council on Aging, "In these types of scams, perpetrators may pose as a Medicare representative to get older people to give them their personal information, or they will provide bogus services for elderly people at makeshift mobile clinics, then use the personal information they provide to bill Medicare and pocket the money."[8]

10. Telemarketing/Phone Scams: I would be hard pressed to find someone who has never had a "cold call." In the real estate industry (at least a few years ago) the figure was that for every 100 calls, there may be three interested in either purchasing or selling a home and you should be able to convince one person that you are the best Realtor for them. Those are not scams, but legitimate calls. Phone blocking that was introduced cut into these calls considerably. Scammers pay no attention to the block. For some reason car and appliance warranty salesperson do not go by the precaution, certainly not the scammers.

The worst scam I remember in the news was someone calling from a foreign country. As they talked to you each minute you were paying an exorbitant amount, such as $1,000 a minute, through the phone company. I have not heard of this one for a while and believe phone companies must have taken some action to stop the practice. The one I remember came from the Dominican Republic.

Tracing scams that do not involve face-to-face contact and have no paper trail are difficult to trace, especially if the home phone does not retain a caller identification phone log digitally. There is one more lingering aftereffect. The buyer's name, I should say scammed person, is also put on a list either for repeat calls, or for other scammers in the dark world of scams.

Some examples of telemarketing fraud are better known by common names like "pigeon drop," "fake accident," "charity, and sweepstakes/lottery winner."[8]

Pigeon Drop: The con artist has come into some big money and for some reason, such as customs, or freezing of assets cannot use it until a "good faith" payment is made to extract the funds. About this time a second con artist gets involved posing as a professional with paper certificates such as a lawyer, banker, refugee politician, or some vague trustworthy stranger. If you will make a deposit (hundreds or thousands of dollars) into their account, they can get the money and split it with you. Note how much this has in common with the Nigerian scams and other African scams on the internet.

Personal story. When I was the first U.S. Department of Commerce Foreign Commercial Officer in Vladivostok Russia as a diplomat, I received a call from Nigeria that said if I sent $10,000, they would be able to purchase part of a producing oilfield that surely would be worth millions to me! Was that brazen or what? A call to me in a Russian Consulate? I am still amazed!

Fake Accident: You receive a frantic call that someone you know is a victim of an accident. They will plead in some convincing ways for you to send money (cash, check, Western Union, PayPal), since the hospital needs it in advance to perform an emergency procedure. I do not know of any hospital that will not provide emergency treatment to anyone including indigents, illegal aliens, or homeless and then seek payment from whatever sources they can including the county if necessary.

Charity Scam: We all know these scams, but our guard is down when there is a natural disaster. Try a hurricane sweeping New Orleans or Houston, a wildfire in California, or a tornado in Kansas. Older people are used to caring and giving. They may not be thinking straight at the time of the call and their emotions have been tapped. For the record, a church is more likely to provide meals and clothing for those struck by a disaster than the Red Cross. That is my opinion based on stories quoted to me and read by me. Furthermore, did you know a "Donation" made through Facebook may have processing fees deducted. If it is a registered charity on the Facebook platform, Facebook will not take out any processing fee.[8] If not a registered charity, "2% of donations are used cover a portion of the costs of nonprofit vetting, security, fraud protection, operational costs, and payment support, 3% of donations go to payment processing...."[11]

Sweepstakes/Lottery Winner Scam: This is another "Big Ticket" scam. It also is related to internet scams that do the same thing, just a different medium. Who does not get excited with the initial exclamation, "You have won $20 million dollars in the Irish Sweepstakes!" There are two problems: you do not remember doing anything to enter the sweepstakes and then the caller says the prize is frozen until you pay $20,000 up front for the fees. Gray Zone citizens, though, of course, not just them alone fall victim and their lives are destroyed. "Inevitably, the caller promises large winnings in exchange for a payment of taxes or fees by the American. In Alexandria, Va., an 85-year-old man lost his home and his life savings. A woman in North Dakota lost more than $300,000. A man in Knoxville, Tenn., committed suicide after sending thousands to a Jamaican group....

Details of a major sting operation from a <u>Washington Post</u> article, February 12, 2019 provide a reason to cheer and clap our hands. It concerns a Jamaican picking the wrong target.

The caller with the Jamaican accent told the 90-year-old District man he had won $72 million and a new Mercedes Benz in the Mega Millions lottery, but the man needed to send $50,000 in taxes and fees to get his money. He also told the Washington man he'd done his research....

"You're a great man," the Jamaican man cajoled. "You was a judge, you was an attorney, you was a basketball player, you were in the U.S. Navy, homeland security. I know everything about you. I even seen your photograph, and I seen your precious wife."

The Jamaican's research didn't turn up everything. He didn't learn that the man he was calling was the former director of the FBI and the CIA, the only person ever to hold both jobs. And he didn't know that William H. Webster would call him back the next day with the FBI listening in. In that reverse sting, Webster obtained the man's real name and email address, while stringing him along and never quite committing to sending the $50,000.

"It's going to take me a few weeks to come up with it," said Webster, also a former federal district and appeals court judge. "I'm as anxious as you are to get the money, but it's going to take me a while to do it," he tells the man on the recorded call that is part of the court record.

"You can pay a part in the meantime," parried the caller, later identified as Keniel A. Thomas.

"How much is a part?" asked Webster.

"You can come with about $20,000 in the meantime," Thomas said.

The conversation was one of many calls that Thomas made to Webster or his wife, Lynda, in 2014, including one in which he promised a bullet "straight to the head" of Lynda.

Thomas was then charged in 2014 with attempted extortion. But Thomas wasn't arrested until late 2017, after he landed in New York on a flight from Jamaica. He pleaded guilty in October and faced a prison term of 33 to 41 months under federal sentencing guidelines. But with Webster and his wife in the courtroom, Chief U.S. District Judge Beryl Howell on Friday added another 2½ years to Thomas's sentence, giving him nearly six years to serve. Howell said that the scam qualified as "organized criminal activity" and that Thomas posed "a threat to a family member of the victim."

"The threat of death to another person is a most serious crime," Webster told the judge, "for which Mr. Thomas is about to pay. ... We truly hope that word has spread into the criminal community of scammers that our Federal Bureau of Investigation and other law enforcement agencies are clamping down on such predatory behaviors."

Jamaican-based telephone scams have mushroomed in recent years, always targeting older or vulnerable Americans and sometimes destroying victims' lives…. Federal authorities pursue the scammers when they can, but extradition from other countries is difficult and prosecution can take years.

The FBI was able to document that Thomas, 29, from St. James Parish in the Montego Bay area, collected at least $300,000 with his scam from about three dozen victims, according to court records. One victim estimated he alone sent Thomas more than $600,000. In order to cover his tracks, Thomas sometimes laundered money through different victims, having one American send money to a second American before it was sent to him in Jamaica. He provided Webster with the name and address of a man in California to whom Thomas wanted Webster to send the money, according to the recorded call Webster made.

The scammers often pass around or sell "lead lists" of potential targets in America, prosecutors told The Washington Post last year, and Lynda Webster said they have continued to receive calls even after Thomas's arrest. The Websters were unlikely to fall for such fraud, "but it's frightening when they talk about putting a bullet in your head," she said Monday."[10]

"Often, seniors will be sent a check that they can deposit in their bank account, knowing that while it shows up in their account immediately, it will take a few days before the (fake) check is rejected. During that time, the criminals will quickly collect money for supposed fees or taxes on the prize, which they pocket while the victim has the "prize money" removed from his or her account as soon as the check bounces.[12]

11. The Grandparent Scam: This scam is the one that plays on the heart strings primarily of Gray Zone citizens. It is not only devious, it is vicious. When the phone is answered, the scam is instantly set in motion, "Hi Grandpa/Grandma, guess who this is." The response is usually with the first name of a grandchild. Thus, with minimal work the scammer established a fake identity with no background research. Initially pleasantries may ensue depending on the skill of the perpetrator. You are the mark and the scam quickly ensues.

The fake grandchild will establish they are in trouble and need money. They are afraid to talk to their parents and need your help. There is a long list of financial problems they may use including trouble with the law like a heavy traffic fine, needing car repairs, or a debt to a friend. Payment is often asked by Western Union or MoneyGram, because they either can use a fake ID based on the name you gave away, or because they often fail to require identification in the first place. Of course, they will conclude with "please don't tell my parents." They can make the need for secrecy even stronger by concluding, "Mom and dad would kill me!"

There is little or no cost to the scammer. While the cost is "only" in the hundreds, they can repeat it over and over with a lot of calls on the same day.

What to Do about Scams

Being proactive in purchasing LifeLock or similar scam protection company easily can be acquired for about $10 per month. They have a guarantee to handle all the problems for you, should they arise, but they "lock out and lock down" your personal information and then have a money guarantee up to $1 million if anything should happen under their protection.

Write down all financial transaction information.

Check with other sources about the legitimacy of the contact(s). If it is a group scam, check outside the group.

In the event you suspect fraud and/or a scam you may contact the local police, your bank if your account is involved or has been compromised, or your credit card company if payment has been made that way. Adult Protective Services (APS) are almost everywhere in every state and city. If you do not know the number, you may call and find out the APS representative in your service area by calling 1-800-677-1116 or by email at https://eldercare.acl.gov. These are federal government sponsored resource lines and they will put you in touch with the appropriate authorities.

As an example, the State of Texas has a state resource agency for reporting abuse of/to seniors. The Texas Department of Family and Protective Services is responsible for investigating abuse, neglect, or exploitation of elderly adults. They also handle the same thing for children and adults with disabilities. If the victim is in a nursing home or an assisted living facility, they should contact the Department of Aging and Disability Services at 1-800-252-2142. If not in a nursing home, then contact Texas Adult Protective Services at 1-800-252-5400.

That is an example of what one state does. There should be similar agencies and departments in every state.

I pointed out these scams to alert Gray Zone members to the common methods of scamming. We are not the only targets, but again I emphasize that we have so much more to lose, especially our savings built over a lifetime of work. I have been one of those watching a lot of scams in operation on television with entire series spent on describing what happened to people personally.

Chapter 4

SOCIAL SECURITY AND RETIREMENT

We have not only an opportunity, but an obligation to get Social Security and Medicare/Medicaid solvent for the next seventy-five years in order that we may restore trust in the system and restrain government efforts to raid it while increasing entitlements for our senior citizens. ~Roy E. Peterson

There are four ways Gray Zone members generally earn money. The obvious one is those who remain in the workforce until retirement. They are continuing contributors to the Social Security Trust Fund who look forward to retirement with or without a separate pension. The intention of the Social Security Act was to provide for those who would not have a separate pension and who were the blue-collar laborers. That changed in a big way as the program morphed over the decades. The second way to earn money is by establishing a business and continuing that business either with direct participation, or by turning over the reins to a trusted partner such as a relative or faithful executive. The third way is to have investments that continue to provide income in retirement. A fourth method is to work either full or part time past retirement. I know some of you bright people out there will come up with several more categories, but they are merely permutations of the four methods I have listed. I know. I considered them myself such as monetizing a hobby, but they all come down to the same four methods, since even work is involved in making and selling a product, or even in writing a book.

Regardless of the method, the middle class has come to rely on Social Security earned entitlements as a primary source of income in retirement. In this chapter you will find that one-third of retirees would be in poverty in their elder years without income from Social Security. I have focused on the issues of Social Security funding and payments. I conclude the chapter with retirement problems. I set aside health issues for a subsequent chapter.

The Social Security Act of 1935, which is Public Law 74-271, was passed under the Administration of President Franklin D. Roosevelt. Although there have been occasional subsequent amendments to the law added and passed by Congress, it remains the basis for retirement and unemployment insurance at the federal level with grants to the states. The benefits paid out under Social Security are called "earned entitlements;" however, with the increasing saddling of the Social Security Trust Fund with other social ills, many of the benefits I argue can no longer be called "earned," but rather welfare payments. Some of them are "gifted welfare programs," as I call them, from the Fund. For the record I use "Social Security Trust Fund" as the easier to recognize nickname of the Old-Age, Survivors, and Disability Insurance (OASDI).

As of 2018, 62 million Americans were drawing Social Security Payments of which 42.8 million were retired workers. This figure comes from the Social Security Administration. What bothers me is the 20 million differential between retired workers and those who receive some form of Social Security funded support. That means one-third who may have partially paid into the system, but for various reasons and sub–title programs like disabilities, blindness, mental health, children left without parents, or even diseases such as Lupus, represent a sizable chunk of people supported by the rest of us. I make no judgment at this point. I merely call your attention to part of the problem. I will provide a list of all the

Title assistance programs that have been added to Social Security over the years in Section 7 below.

There are seven issues that rile retirees and that those in, or approaching the Gray Zone need to take up and make political tests for electing members of Congress. These issues are: 1.) Lump Sum Death Benefit remaining the same low amount of $255 for decades and no longer paid either to surviving children or as was formerly the case, claimed as partial payment by the funeral home. 2.) Taxation of Social Security when a retiree earns above a tiered threshold for income tax purposes. 3.) The last check syndrome, as I call it, that often is the final payment made by the administration, but does not cover the end of life of some and must be repaid even if sent to their account. 4.) Medicare deduction from annual Social Security payments. 5.) Recent attempts to raid the Social Security Trust Fund. 6.) Cost of Living Allowance. 7.) Securing the future of the Social Security Trust Fund. This is the section division for the chapter. I add at the end an eighth section that offers Debatable Propositions for Social Security reform.

Lump Sum Death Benefit (LDSB)

You may or may not agree that the LDSB should be raised to at least cover the cost of cremation, which at a minimum is $600, although that price moves up to $1,500 to $2,000 depending on the city, state, and funeral home. In any event I take issue with the $255 being the maximum paid by the Social Security Administration as a death benefit, especially when I found out that I could not claim it when my mother dies, since the rules had been changed that only a spouse could receive the death benefit!

When the Social Security Act was passed, Congress did not even have the foresight to realize that a high percentage of spouses would use the payment to pay funeral expenses. That essentially is what it has become. During the intervening years, the Social Security Administration allowed the benefit to be paid directly to the funeral home that made a claim for partial payment of a funeral. That changed with an Omnibus Budget Reconciliation Act passed in 1981, that stated the only ones eligible to receive the payment were spouses of the deceased if living with the retiree or worker at the time of death, or a spouse or child receiving monthly benefits based on the worker's record.[1]

When originally established in the 1935 Social Security Act, the LSDB was not thought of as payment for a funeral, but as a one-time benefit to the survivor. The maximum that could be paid at the time was $315, though the average paid out by 1939 was $96.93. A 1950 Amendment raised the amount based on a formula and that in turn was changed to a maximum of $255 in 1954.[1] 1954?! That number has not changed for 65 years! By contrast Veterans Administration pays burial allowances in cash to the family of an eligible veteran to directly defray burial and funeral costs. These are described as two payments: 1.) A burial (cremated or not) and 2.) a plot interment allowance. The payments for a non-service death (think of that as retirees or those with prior service) of $300 funeral and burial expenses and $780 for a plot.[2] There are various adjustments, such as paying more for the death of an indigent veteran with no apparent relatives.

At least the Veterans Administration had a better idea of what a death benefit should be. Congress should be made to rethink the LSDB and base it on some limited funeral and burial plot number that makes sense. Certainly, that number is nowhere near $255!

I conducted some research on the cost of cremation versus the cost of burial with services when my own wife passed away. In my city the lowest cost for cremation was $600, but ranged up to $2,000 for the exact same thing, ashes in a decorative vase. The cost for a full-scale funeral viewing, transportation to a grave site, and burial, averaged about $7,500 using even the lowest cost casket, though not a wooden container.

The editor of Funeral Online covered some surveys that showed wild deviation in funeral, burial, and cremation costs. Writing in July 1918, Sara Marsden noted cost for cremation varied "significantly."[3] That made it virtually impossible to compare; however, I assert that establishing a new base would pull the high costs down as long as they could count on payment from the Social Security Administration at some support level. As Marsden stated, "Even within a state or city the cost for cremation can differ $100's or even $1,000's."[3] She cited an efuneral survey that included the Cremation Association of North America (CANA). CANA claimed that "the national average cost of a cremation is $1,650." This covered basics only. From their own research by Funeral Online, that said DFS Memorial network conducted a separate survey of low-cost cremation services, they determined that "the price for cremation services can differ by as much as over $2,000 for the exact same cremation service.[3]

Clearly $255 does not cut it either as an income replacement as was the original intent, or as any kind of burial costs as it became for a time. The military concept is at least a much more informed approach by separating burial expenses from plot costs and providing a little over $1,000 to take care of the problem.

What is the problem Congress? Private insurance companies that want everyone to make payments to them? Failure to understand the final expense costs or pay attention to families that cannot afford them? You have not even thought of establishing another separate fund like Medicare or Medicaid to assist, although you did that with a lot of other programs that burden the fund. You do realize it could be a small added deduction from somewhere in the wages or benefits paid out!

Potential Taxation of a Portion of the Earned Entitlements

In the beginning Social Security was not taxed. The reason is explained by Social Security Historian, Larry DeWitt: "At the time, the Treasury Department issued specific tax rulings that made it clear that Social Security benefits were excluded from federal income taxation.... the Treasury considered the benefits to be gifts, rejecting the idea that they were directly tied to the payroll taxes that funded the benefits. That made sense at the time, since workers paying into the system for the first time were not yet eligible for benefits, and those retirees who could get Social Security generally hadn't paid much in payroll taxes."[4]

My first thought is why did Congress not put that in the original legislation? My second thought was how could this provision be a decision left to the Treasury Department? It seems to be an important distinction!

For 48 years from the inception of Social Security with passage of the 1935 Social Security Act until 1983, Social Security payments were not taxed at all. According to the Social Security Administration Historian, "Since a pair of 1938 Treasury Department Tax Rulings, and another in 1941, Social Security benefits have been explicitly excluded from federal income taxation. (A revision was issued in 1970, but it made no changes in the existing policy.) This changed for the first time with the passage of the 1983 Amendments to the Social Security Act. Beginning in 1984, a portion of Social Security benefits have been subject to federal income taxes."[4]

"Starting in 1979, an advisory council on Social Security reform suggested taxing 50% of Social Security benefits, arguing that was more in line with how other types of retirement-related income got taxed. Lawmakers didn't like the idea of imposing tax on every retiree, so they proposed letting low-income retirees be exempt from the measure."[4]

"Further recommendations came in the early 1980s from future Federal Reserve chair **Alan Greenspan**'s National Commission on Social Security Reform, which adopted a similar methodology to what had been proposed early on. In the end, the rules that lawmakers adopted in 1983 forced Social Security recipients to include some of their Social Security benefits in taxable income if their "combined income" -- that is, their **adjusted gross income** on their tax return plus tax-exempt bond interest and one-half of their annual Social Security benefits -- was higher than $25,000 for single filers or $32,000 for joint filers."[4]

"The Senate Finance Committee Report offered these additional observations: '. . . *by taxing social security benefits and appropriating these revenues to the appropriate trust funds, the financial solvency of the social security trust funds will be strengthened. . .. By taxing only a portion of social security and railroad retirement benefits (that is, up to one-half of benefits in excess of a certain base amount), the Committee's bill assures that lower-income individuals . . . will not be taxed on their benefits. The maximum proportion of benefits taxed is one-half in recognition of the fact that social security benefits are partially financed by after-tax employee contributions.*'"[4]

Goodness knows that the costs of medicine and medical assistance, not to mention hospice care or senior care facilities, have increased and outpaced medical insurance plans, Medicare and Medicaid costs that may require copay, and drugs that are only partially covered in some cases. The health care system that was mandated and is now in the process of being revamped did not solve the entire problem either. Why must taxes be paid on any portion of retired Social Security earned entitlements?

Not only can they be taxed by the federal government, but they can also be taxed by state governments as can a pension, even a military one! That is also unacceptable by the way! Congress giveth and then taketh away! The reason they began doing it was fears of the Social Security Trust Fund running out of money in the 1980's.[5] That is all well and good, but to look to get back a portion of Social Security is not! It should be sacrosanct and set aside! Not a piggybank.

The present taxation level could reach 85% on Social Security as we are operating from the final revisions of tax thresholds and levels made way back in 1993! While there is a COLA increase in place at a modest average of around 2.5%, though some years it is rated at zero increase, the broad costs on which it is based have no relation to the runaway costs of medicines, medical care, and either in home or resident care facilities! Gray Zone citizens have increasingly had to work until the age of 70! If they take their maximum Social Security at that age the average recipient will receive $1,461 per month in 2019. Without it, millions of seniors would be sinking, especially since savings are often zero when they retire. The payment is supposed to equal 40% of income prior to retirement, but studies have found it usually takes 80% to survive at a decent level.[6] That means alternative methods are needed to earn money at an age when employment opportunities are limited, skills are greatly diminished, capabilities have eroded, and mental acuity is not as great. Social Security was not meant to replace retirement funds, but in fact millions have lost their pensions as they near their retirement goal and savings are nil. Currently 20 million Gray Zone members must pay taxes on a portion of their Social Security payments.[5]

I find this ridiculous, especially since they have to pay on their income they make by separate means, whether a retirement pension from the private sector or from the government, as well.

Last Check Syndrome

I call the last check issued to a deceased recipient a "syndrome," because it put me in one. When my mother died, it was the 18th of December 2015. She was one of those who received her payment on the third Wednesday of the month. That was on the 16th, two days prior. I had her senior care facility for which I needed to pay her stay for the first eighteen days of the month. With the total care cost per month having sharply risen over the previous five years to $5,000 per month, I was barely able to cover monthly expenses and in fact with the increase that year ran out of her savings with medicine counted separately.

I counted on the Social Security payment, but the Social Security Administration demanded repayment of the December check, which I negotiated to do at $100 per month. First the bad news, I had to repay the entire check. Now for the "good" news. They were flexible enough to allow repayment over time. I was caught half way between angry and relieved. If I felt that way, image the millions facing the same issue and the anger that must cause throughout the electorate. I specially added electorate, since this apparently can only be remedied by the electorate!

Medicare Deduction from Earned Entitlements

Can someone explain to me why my Medicare deduction from my "benefits" was $1,768 for 2019? I paid into Medicare for a long time. It was taken out of my paychecks. Now if you think you can explain that, why the double taxation? Oh, I know, it is counted as an added benefit and goes into my Income Tax Calculation raising the amount on which any taxes must be paid if I go over a threshold or two? Wait! Something is still wrong! Not only that, but the cost has gone out of sight compared to when I first began.

I know it can be explained using the same thought that the Alan Greenspan Commission used about private sources of income, but perceptually I still feel used and abused! I should not have to pay anything for Medicare when I am in my retirement and least able to afford it. Make another note for the electorate to change things.

Attempts to Raid the Trust Fund

For the 2018 election, I became angry that members of Congress were attempting to raid the Social Security Trust Fund to help defray other government expenses! I learned my own Republic Representative from here in Texas voted for the shifting of funds. I became even more aggravated when I discovered his profession had been an accountant for the Bush clan in Midland. When I discovered this, the primaries had already been conducted. I threw my hat in the ring as the Write-in candidate and attempted to work through a social media platform; however, I knew I was exceedingly late. I am still perturbed.

In my opinion, the Social Security Trust Fund is off limits to the greedy hands of government! Then they have the nerve to tell me the fund is going to run dry by the year 2035 as currently projected, if nothing is done. "After this point, retirees can generally expect about 75 cents on every dollar of their scheduled benefits."[7]

Scare tactics work well on the elderly. Those of us in the Gray Zone want to make sure the fund lasts not only as long as we do, but as long as our children do. That requires an adjustment to their tax shoulders, not ours. Of course, I could cite former ancient Senator Alan Simpson of Wyoming who thought our generation is already too greedy.

Cost of Living Allowance (COLA)

The Cost of Living Allowance (COLA) was introduced in the Social Security Act Amendments of 1950. These amendments raised benefits and put the program "on the road to the virtually universal coverage it has today."[8]

As I already mentioned though, COLA is based on a broad amount of data, which is somewhat helpful, but does not account for the rocketing costs of medicines and medical care, and then there are senior citizen facilities whose average costs vary considerably from state to state as shown in the Genworth's Cost of Care Survey below.[9]

Table 3-1: Shared Average Room Costs

State	Daily	Monthly	Yearly
Alabama	$95	$2,900	$34,800
Alaska	$189	$5,750	$69,000
Arizona	$115	$3,500	$42,000
Arkansas	$103	$3,133	$37,590
California	$132	$4,000	$48,000
Colorado	$134	$4,063	$48,750
Connecticut	$163	$4,950	$59,400
Delaware	$176	$5,368	$64,416
District of Columbia	$220	$6,700	$80,400
Florida	$100	$3,045	$36,540
Georgia	$94	$2,850	$34,200
Hawaii	$136	$4,125	$49,500
Idaho	$105	$3,200	$38,400
Illinois	$128	$3,898	$46,770
Indiana	$116	$3,528	$42,330
Iowa	$116	$3,518	$42,210
Kansa	$127	$3,863	$46,350
Kentucky	$108	$3,300	$39,600
Louisiana	$104	$3,155	$37,860
Maine	$164	$4,991	$59,892
Maryland	$123	$3,750	$45,000
Massachusetts	$180	$5,463	$65,550
Michigan	$117	$3,563	$42,750
Minnesota	$105	$3,200	$38,400
Mississippi	$105	$3,200	$38,400
Missouri	$83	$2,537	$30,438
Montana	$115	$3,513	$42,150
Nebraska	$115	$3,510	$42,120
Nevada	$100	$3,050	$36,600
New Hampshire	$158	$3,600	$43,200

New Jersey	$163	$4,950	$59,400
New Mexico	$118	$3,600	$43,200
New York	$136	$4,136	$49,635
North Carolina	$99	$3,000	$36,000
North Dakota	$110	$3,340	$40,080
Ohio	$118	$3,600	$43,200
Oklahoma	$92	$2,803	$33,630
Oregon	$134	$4,065	$48,780
Pennsylvania	$118	$3,600	$43,200
Rhode Island	$162	$4,931	$59,161
South Carolina	$99	$3,000	$36,000
South Dakota	$111	$3,370	$40,440
Tennessee	$124	$3,780	$45,360
Texas	$116	$3,515	$42,180
Utah	$97	$2,950	$35,400
Vermont	$160	$4,860	$58,320
Virginia	$130	$3,950	$47,400
Washington	$148	$4,500	$54,000
West Virginia	$107	$3,263	$39,150
Wisconsin	$129	$3,934	$47,205
Wyoming	$131	$3,995	$47,940

My problem with the costs is they exceed entitlements paid by a few thousand dollars, depending on the state, Social Security payments. This is where Senators and Representatives in Congress scoff and try to paint a rosy picture that the states can use their block grants to make up the difference if the Gray Zone citizens have no further resources. They can also use their savings or separate retirement pensions. This is where I tell them that social welfare programs such as these cause them to have to get a divorce from their long-term spouse so that they can qualify for the welfare. Heaven help them if there is an ice cream bar or soda machine. Where do they get the money for such minimal comforts? I remember my dad asked me for money so he could purchase soft drinks from a vending machine in the hallway of the facility where he and my mother stayed. Come now Congress. Either change the laws to allow a few bucks at least to be available for discretionary spending on treats or take outs from restaurants, or make it be included in the price of the stay.

Securing the Trust Fund for the Future

Given the importance of Social Security earned entitlements for the Gray Zone not being diminished, but rather extended by COLA and other means, such as elimination of the tax altogether, securing the OASDI (Social Security) Trust Fund is one of the most important things Congress can do to reassure our age group and garner votes. First, we have to raise the issues to an overwhelming level of national urgency and importance.

I understand the arguments citing we have almost $3 Trillion in the Trust Fund, so why hurry? Any surplus income by the way was to have been properly invested in securities according to mandates of the law. I would like to see an audit of what is going on with our money! Wouldn't you?

A. Factors.

There are at least five major factors than impinge on the stability of the fund for the coming decades. 1.) Baby Boomers. 2.) Increased Longevity. 3.) Federal Reserve Policies. 4) Abortions 5.) Adding Programs

1.) Baby Boomers: Everyone recognizes the Baby Boomer Bulge, so to speak. For a decade it has been impacting Social Security funds. What has changed is the ratio of workers who are paying into the system is losing ground to the beneficiary eligible Boomers.

2.) Longevity: When Social Security first came into existence, the legislators, or at least those who prepared the legislation envisioned its purpose as providing what has been termed, "the safety net" mainly for low income workers for only a few years of retirement. The Social Security Administration and the Bureau of Statistics report, however, that since 1960, average life expectancy in the United States rose about nine years. This longevity obviously means a longer payout period than ever envisioned.

3.) Federal Reserve: The drop and consistently low interest of the Fed means that the special-issue bonds into which Social Security reserves have been going receive a concomitantly low interest rate for the surplus funds.

4.) Abortions: I have not seen anyone else take abortions into account; however, no one can deny that native born American citizens not being allowed to mature and go to work negatively affects the worker force. The totals reported to the Centers for Disease Control and Prevention from 1970 to 2015 were more than 45 million. A large portion of those would have entered the work force and the economy both as wage earners and spenders. That would have provided a major boost to the Social Security system over three decades from 1970 to 2000. Some would be in college and some killed, but a large number would also have become wage earners over the next fifteen years as reported. See the table below.[13]

Table 3-2: Abortions Reported to the CDC Per Year[11]

Year	#CDC	Year	#CDC	Year	#CDC	Year	#CDC
1980	1,297,606	1990	1,429,247	2000	857,475	2010	765,651
1981	1,300,980	1991	1,388,937	2001	853,485	2111	730,322
1982	1,303,980	1992	1,359,145	2002	854,122	2112	699,202
1983	1,268,987	1993	1,330,414	2003	848,163	2113	664,435
1984	1,333,521	1994	1,267,415	2004	839,226	2114	652,639
1985	1,328,570	1995	1,210,883	2005	820,151	2115	638,169
1986	1,328,112	1996	1,221,585	2006	852,385	2116	SNC
1987	1,353,671	1997	1,186,039	2007	827,609	2117	SNC
1988	1,371,285	1998	884,273	2008	825,564	2118	SNC
1989	1,186,039	1999	861,789	2009	789,507	2019	x

Numbers not completed yet for 2016-18.

The CDC numbers are not complete. They do not include California, Florida, Maryland, New Hampshire and Wyoming because they either "did not report, did not report by age, or did not meet reporting standards," the CDC report said.)[17]

5.) Adding Programs Originally Not Intended for Social Security: I get it! The safest place for Congress to park Socialist welfare programs is under the banner of Social Security. Tell me that does not drain the Social Security Fund of its surpluses over time and increase the amounts from paychecks that go to pay for the programs. Before the left and other meaning well citizens, start banging their fists on the table and tell me we have to do it for compassion and other reasons, I actually support a means to help citizens that are in trouble through no fault of their own and who have worked to put money into the system. I just don't want them to continue by adding more programs into Social Security and I want them to remove the ones that do not belong here, but in a separate welfare program.

It began with the Social Security Amendments of 1965 that are codified as H.R. 7544, October 24, 1963, Public Law 88-156, Title XVII.[11] Here are all the programs now under the umbrella of Social Security:

Title I	Grants to States for Old-Age Assistance for the Aged.
Title II	Federal Old-Age, Survivors, and Disability Insurance Benefits.
Title III	Grants to States for Unemployment Compensation Administration.
Title IV	Grants to States for Aid and Services to Needy Families with Children and for Child-Welfare

Services.

<u>Title V</u>	Maternal and Child Health Services Block Grant.
<u>Title VI</u>	Temporary State Fiscal Relief.
<u>Title VII</u>	Administration.
<u>Title VIII</u>	Special Benefits for Certain World War II Veterans.
<u>Title IX</u>	Miscellaneous Provisions Relating to Employment Security
<u>Title X</u>	Grants to States for Aid to the Blind
<u>Title XI</u>	General Provisions, Peer Review, and Administrative Simplification
<u>Title XII</u>	Advances to State Unemployment Funds
<u>Title XIII</u>	Reconversion Unemployment Benefits for Seamen
<u>Title XIV</u>	Grants to States for Aid to the Permanently and Totally Disabled
<u>Title XV</u>	Unemployment Compensation for Federal Employees
<u>Title XVI</u>	Grants to States for Aid to the Aged, Blind, or Disabled
<u>Title XVI</u>	Supplemental Security Income for the Aged, Blind, and Disabled
<u>Title XVII</u>	Grants for Planning Comprehensive Action to Combat Mental Retardation
<u>Title XVIII</u>	Health Insurance for the Aged and Disabled
<u>Title XIX</u>	Grants to States for Medical Assistance Programs
<u>Title XX</u>	Block Grants to States for Social Services

<u>Title XXI</u>   State Children's Health Insurance Program

You may go to the Social Security Administration and consult each one of these titles. This table is not found in a Table of Contents, but was generated separately.

There are other less important factors and then there are some specious claims that do not fit the overall argument. One of those I read was income inequality means the rich live longer and strain the program; however, under the present system of taxation that does not hold water and I would argue it is irrelevant in the first place for many reasons.

The importance of Social Security cannot be overestimated in keeping Gray Zone members out of poverty. In 2016, the Center for Budget Policies and Priorities found "that Social Security's guaranteed monthly payout ensures that 22.1 million people…are kept out of poverty."[12]

B. Projections.

Sean Williams writing in <u>The Motley Fool</u> describes a major change coming in 2022. This change is projected based on intermediate-cost forecasts of the Social Security Trust Fund.

He takes his case from the Social Security Board of Trustees' 2017 report. As reported by the Social Security Administration, current asset reserves have grown to $2.9 Trillion and is scheduled soon to reach the $3 Trillion figure.[12]

By now one begins to think that since the fund continues to grow reserve assets that program should be good for another 50-years at least. So why are fund watchers sounding the alarm that the fund will run out? If there are fears about it running out, why doesn't Congress do something about it now?

You may not remember this, but I do. George W. Bush was concerned about the fund running out soon and made it one of his priorities to get Congress to solve during his Presidency. Like a lot of things such as solving illegal immigration by passing legislation, the subject of Social Security solvency is a can that keeps getting kicked down the road. The attitude is if it does not have a political impact on me and if the elephant in the room is far down the path and half hidden in the forest, why bother? Let subsequent Congresses solve the problem.

Returning to the 2017 report from the Board of Trustees who employed what they term an "intermediate-cost forecast model," they projected net increases and net decreases to the program through 2026 as follows:

Table3-3: Projected Social Security Fund Annually Increases or Decreases[12]

Year	Amount in Billions	Increase/ Decease
2017	$58.6	Increase
2018	$44.7	Increase
2019	$29.3	Increase
2020	$16.8	Increase
2021	$3.3	Increase
2022	$18.2	Decrease
2023	$46.4	Decrease
2024	$75.7	Decrease
2025	$108.9	Decrease
2026	$143.8	Decrease

Making the calculations, the author notes "By 2026, not only will Social Security's asset reserves be depleted by almost $395 billion from their peak in 2021, but the trust fund ratio...of asset reserves relative to scheduled benefits to be paid, will have fallen from 298% in 2017 to just 165% in 2026."[12]

One can just look at the specter of diminishing funds beginning in 2022 and conclude the time to solve the problem (again) is now. Since I am writing this in 2019, the time is even closer by three years than the report projections from 2016. So, what are the options for securing Social Security into the future? The options seem simple: increase the methods of funding and/or decrease benefits.

C. Methods to Solve the Problem.

Short of transferring money in from the General Fund, which is one future option should Congress not have solved the problem by then and should the fund be insolvent, there presently are three ways the Trust Fund is fed money: a.) Payroll taxes. b.) Interest on surplus assets (reserves). c.) Taxes on benefits.

1. Funding Increase Methods:

a. Payroll taxes: Payroll taxes provide the primary source of income to the Trust Fund. The tax rate remains as it has for some years at 12.4% This is based on 6.2% for the employer and 6.2% taken from the wages of the worker. Payroll Tax accounted for $836.2 billion which was 87.3% of Trust Fund income of $957.5 billion collected in 2016. making it obviously the most important contributor.[10]

As mentioned in the National Committee for the Preservation of Social Security and Medicare (NCPSSM) report of the highlights of the 2018 Summary Report of the Trust Fund, "As long as the payroll tax remains the primary funding mechanism for Social Security, and Americans keep working, the program will collect revenue that can be disbursed to eligible beneficiaries. This ensures that the program can't go bankrupt."[14] That should be reassuring;

however, future losses over time would mean future cuts in benefits.

b. Interest income on surplus assets (reserves): This figure was $88.4 Billion in 2016[10] and $85 billion in 2017. This is 8.54%[14]

Federal Reserve special note interest rates marginally increased in 2018 and are likely to hold steady through 2019. This is the second most important contributor to the fund.

c. Taxes of Social Security benefits themselves: In 2016, "taxation of the benefits generated $32.8 billion."[10] The percent of income for the Social Security Fund in 2017 was 3.8% of total income.[14] This is the category that I personally would like to see removed, since it hits the middle class the hardest.

2. Benefit Cuts:

This option is going to be dead on arrival at Congressional Committees unless they want to commit political suicide. There is enough outrage in 2019 at not receiving sufficient raises in the COLA and deducting both for taxes depending on the level of extraneous income and for Medicare that Gray Zone citizens all thought had been paid through their previous taxes.

Benefit cuts are not a real option in my opinion. Cutting benefits by what some projections suggest of 23% to 25 %, would plunge millions into poverty, cause a political insurrection, and change the political landscape. So far, as studies have pointed out, workers are willing to have increased percentages taken from salaries in order to ensure future viability of Social Security.

D. State of the Social Security Fund as of 2019

I have already used some of the statistics from the NCPSSM Highlights of the most recent Social Security Trust

Fund (June 2018); however, a short review and summary of their document provides a solid base for discussion and comment. My basic takeaway from their report is Social Security remains stable and strong.[14]

I learned in doing research that the Trust Fund each year surveys and projects 75 years out from the date of the analysis.[14] There are assumptions built into the report concerning bond payment rates, health of the economy, workers in the work force contributing, longevity of Gray Zone citizens, the only changes to benefits are COLA raises, and no further programs of welfare are added to the system.

With those thoughts in mind I will use some of data and information in the report further:

1. Benefits: Full benefits as they are will last until 2034, fifteen years from now without cuts in the program. Cuts in the program as I have stated are political poison, or at least should be for Gray Zone segment of the population.

2. **Reserves:** "The Trustees report there is now $2.89 trillion in the Social Security Trust Fund, which is $44 billion more than last year, and that these reserves will continue to contribute to the funding of the program, yielding interest income of about $85 billion per year."[14]

3. **Actuarial Deficit:** "The 2018 report finds that the combined OASDI Trust Fund has an actuarial deficit equal to 2.84 percent of payroll, barely changed from the 2.83 percent shortfall projected last year."[14] Note that this is using the payroll contribution figure only, not the reserves and taxes on benefits. This suggests to me that a raise of 1.4% on each side of the contributory ledger (employer/worker) split would be a great fix to introduce now and that means the Trust Fund reserves would either continue to grow or sometime after 2034 would only slowly deteriorate. While the NCPSSM suggests

that lifting the payroll tax cap on benefits, I suggest that other fixes could eliminate the tax altogether on Social Security benefits."[14]

4. Recipients: "At the end of 2017, about 62 million people were receiving benefits: 45.5 million retired workers and their dependents, 6 million survivors of deceased workers, and 10.4 million disabled workers and their dependents."[14]

5. Worker Contributors: "About 173 million workers had earnings covered by Social Security and paid payroll taxes."[14]

6. General Fund Payments: Less than 1% annually is attributed to miscellaneous inputs from the General Fund.

7. Suggested New COLA Index Needed: The National Committee reinforced my contention that COLA needs to be strengthened because of the factors affecting income of those in the Gray Zone. COLA is based on inflation to be sure; however, as I pointed out and later discovered in the National Committee Report:

"The National Committee believes that this estimate does not accurately reflect the inflation affecting today's seniors and believes that Social Security's COLA needs to be strengthened.....The Social Security COLA is based on the Bureau of Labor Statistics measurement of the increase in the cost of a market basket of goods and services from the third quarter of one year to the third quarter of the next year.....(however) Seniors spend a significant portion of their income on out-of-pocket health care expenses not covered by Medicare. As time goes by, more and more of their Social Security benefit checks will be eaten up by rising health care costs. According to the Medicare Trustees, 35 percent of the

Debatable Propositions for Social Security Reform

1. Eliminate Taxes on Earned Entitlements (Benefits): I understand the desire to tax those that make certain thresholds of income from other sources, but keep the tax on that income, not on earned entitlements.

2. Change the Basis for COLA Calculation: As pointed out in the National Committee report, using an index for COLA based on the "market basket" of goods and services to keep up with inflation is inadequate. The recommendation is for a more highly developed, specific index for the elderly taking into account the continuing rise in medical care, drug prescription increases, and senior care facility rising costs. I contend senior buying power has already eroded and needs to be fixed.

3. Lump Sum Death Benefit Increase and Change: The LSDB has remained the same for seven decades at $255 or less as it was in the beginning. This sum should be allowed to be made to the primary inheritor, not just a spouse and it needs to be raised to a respectable level, which I argued is $1,000 in 2019.

4. Last Check Payment: Like the LSDB, the final check should never leave out half those who die in a particular month. Payment must be allowed through the end of the month when a person becomes deceased.

5. End Medicare Deduction from Earned Entitlement: This is one of those hidden mirror tricks in the system. That burden has been paid for by now by those who have worked in the economy. This burden that dramatically reduces entitlements such as in my case by about $150 per month, must be removed. For those whose only income is entitlements and those on marginal income above Social Security, this clearly is unacceptable.

6. Increase Payroll Taxes by 1.4% each on the Employer and Worker Sides: This would ensure solvency for an even greater extended time without even dipping into reserves.

7. Seal Social Security from further Welfare Programs: If Congress ever seeks to add another program here such as some kind of additional insurance, the new program must be fully funded and pay for itself. I recommend a separate welfare system that already exists such as food stamps and that no further programs be added to Social Security.

8. Seal Social Security from Government Borrowing: In 2017 or 2018, off the top of my head, Congress tried to borrow billions from the Trust Fund. While they may have had the aim of paying it back with interest, there already is a Federal Reserve system in place that pays into the reserves by purchasing bonds. Taking more money out in anyway is a huge perceptual problem.

Confidence in the Social Security system must be maintained at all costs.

9. Specify No Payments to Illegal Immigrants: I found no provisions for eliminating payments to illegal immigrants in the Social Security Acts. That must be made explicit with a provision for restitution by any discovered illegally receiving such payments either through a Deferred Action for Childhood Arrivals (DACA) child, or any other method with the DACA child as the guarantor of repayment. This will also depend, of course, on the future legal status of DACA's.

10. Stiffen Penalties for Social Security Number Theft and Misuse: Theft or misuse of Social Security is fraud and has a current penalty in 2019 of not more than $5,000 for each benefit received during the commission of the fraud. The Commissioner of Social Security may bar a medical provider or doctor from further participation in any of the Title XVIII programs.[15]

There are several types of fraud: a.) Furnishing false identifying information on a Social Security application, b.) Furnishing false information to increase Social Security payments, c.) Making a false statement about the amount of wages and period of time they were paid, d.) Using another person's Social Security payment.

The first recommendation would be to make specific jail time required in addition to the civil penalties. A second one would add use in voter fraud with a heavy penalty attached to the crime.

Added Observations and Problems

Besides these ten recommendations there are some observations on problems with suggested solutions.

1. Card Security: The Social Security card provided appears to easily be fabricated. It is not even enclosed in plastic laminate with holograms. A major overhaul could provide an excellent opportunity to track card users, identify illegal users, and make it a requirement for presentation for voting both at registration and at the booth. Computers must be sophisticated enough by now to check glitches and anomalies.

2. National Identification Card: The Social Security Card is the de facto National Identification Card. Most countries have such a card in place. Originally it was political anathema, since it seemed it would impact personal privacy. That train has long since left the station with cell phones, ubiquitous closed-circuit cameras, driver licenses, and other social devices and media. The Social Security Cards would gradually be issued through local police or state departments of motor vehicles with the requirement of proof of residency and proof of citizenship. Once upon a time I might have recommended extended use of state issued driver licenses, but California and other states have subverted that process by giving cards to illegal aliens.

Fixing the Future

Clearly something must be done to fix Social Security for the future. The debatable propositions I suggested must be taken seriously and incorporated into Social Security reform at the earliest possible time. It does not take a crystal ball to foresee the need for change. The only question is how much of a crisis will it take to change the future without sudden kneejerk responses as the deadline for the fixes looms larger and larger. I noted that George Bush pushed for fixes in the early part of his administration and that was 18 years ago.

I expected taking care of the Gray Zone would become a major issue in the 2020 campaign for the Presidency and Congress. In 2017 and 2018 I sent comments by email to the national party committees and a few members of Congress from my state of Texas, that whichever party decides to improve Social Security by extending its solvency for a lengthy period of time and providing increases for "annuitants," would sweep the election, depending on how bad a party stumbled or succeeded on other issues. I have my doubts that those emails ever got past the gatekeeper readers at the other end, by I was sounding an alarm and providing what I considered to be the single biggest voter winner.

As I was completing this chapter on the last day before my future editing, I became aware that Democrats in the House of Representatives have a bill in the works essentially doing some of the things I have listed, namely extension of solvency through an increase in worker payments plus making those above the threshold of $132,900 (2019 level) pay in at the same rate on all their additional earned income (obviously a socialist pitch) and increasing entitlement payments to recipients. According to the article 200 lawmakers in the House have sign on in agreement.[18]

The Democratic sponsored bill suggests gradually increasing payroll contributions for both workers and employers over time, in this case 2043 from 6.2 percent to 7.4 percent for each for a total of 14.8 percent.[18] You will discover this close to my original proposal above in paragraph 6, "Debatable Propositions." Gradual increase makes a lot of sense as suggested in the present form of the sponsored bill.

The author of the article used the term expansion of the program, but reading the script what is under consideration is changing the formula for COLA calculation to increase payments for the present entitled set, which as you have noted was one of my planks in Social Security reform. According to the article, the Social Security Administration "would use a different formula to determine annual bumps intended to more accurately reflect (reflects sic) rising costs for older Americans. Additionally, the bill also would create a new minimum benefit set at 125 percent of the poverty line and take other steps to ease financial pressure on retirees, including doubling the amount of Social Security income that isn't subject to taxation."[18] The bill is title Social Security 2100, which is no accident, since, as I said, the goal of any Social Security Legislation comes from the original mandate of taking care of 75 years ahead.

Those who object to such changes and increases for the Gray Zone always contemplate the impact on savings and levels of poverty of present workers; however, in my opinion future benefits are much more important to extended life expectancy and survival. They also suggest fewer will save money, since Social Security would replace other retirement de facto in the long run.

Make up your own mind on Social Security issues. I believe that this chapter will have a significant impact on anyone who reads it. Logic must prevail, otherwise we all will be sunk together.

What can each of us do about the subject?

My first effort is to complete this book on time so that the issues are clear in voters' minds. I believe that the next election (2020) will be another major milestone with five priority issues determining the outcome of the election for each political party. Those issues in my perceived order of priority are 1.) Homeland Security and Illegal Immigration, 2.) Health Policy, 3.) Social Security Reform, 4.) Voter Fraud and identification of legal voters, and 5.) Rise of Socialist Concepts. In my mind Gray Zone voters and those closely allied with them will make Social Security Reform the balancer and tipping scale for election.

Second, I plan on sending this chapter to the relevant Social Security Legislators beginning with the House Ways and Means Committee, Subcommittee on Social Security and the United States Senate Finance Subcommittee on Social Security, Pensions, and Family Policy.

John Larson (D, CT) sits on the House Ways and Means Committee and chairs the Subcommittee on Social Security. The other members are:

Tom Reed II (R, NY) as ranking member.
Jody Arrington (R, TX)
Brendan Boyle (D, PA)
Ron Estes (R, KS)
Drew Ferguson (R, GA)
Brian Higgins (D, NY)
Daniel Kildee (D, MI)
Bill Pascrell (D, NJ)
Bradley Schneider (D, IL)
Linda Sanchez (D, CA)

Of course, the House Subcommittee presently is controlled by the Democrats and the responsible Senate Subcommittee is controlled by the Republicans. Rob Portman (R, OH) sits as the Chairman of the Social Security, Pensions, and Family Policy Subcommittee. The members of that committee are:

Chuck Grassley (R, IA)
Bill Cassidy (R, LA)
Pat Toomey (R, PA)
James Lankford (R, OK)
Todd Young (R, IN)
Sherrod Brown (D, OH) Ranking Member
Michael F. Bennet (D, CO)
Bob Casey, Jr. (D, PA)

I suggest everyone communicate with your legislative representatives in the U.S. House and Senate. It is particularly incumbent on us all also to communicate our wishes to the two subcommittees, especially those who have them as their direct representatives.

There presently are two more bills of importance to the Gray Zone:

Senate bill S1255 which would amend title II to credit caregivers of dependent relatives with deemed wages up to five years of such service and support State medical training programs for caregivers. Here we go with expansion without further funding sources yet. With the proposed revisions of the previous bill to provide the sources, you have to decide whether or not it should be expanded.[19] My debatable proposition was to seal Social Security from plunder in the future.

House of Representatives bill HR 5768 would amend the Social Security Act to improve access to diabetes outpatient self-management training services, and for other purposes. I say other purposes because these are in flux.[19] The same issues raised in my debatable propositions applies.

Chapter 5

HEALTH ISSUES AND POLITICS

How old would you be if you didn't know how old you was?
~Satchel Paige (1906-1982) Former Major League Pitcher.

Gray Zone citizens are not alone in being concerned about health issues. We have that in common with every segment of society, however, there are problems that inordinately fall into our sphere of experience and competence. Whether it is pain impacting us, Alzheimer's facing us, care giving in an institution or at home, the high costs of prescriptions and medical care, or all of the above, we need to cope, survive, and receive the care needed. Fortunately, we have lived in a society that still cares what happens to the elderly, but that may not always be the case. That is why we have to act now to insure our future by legislation that is passed and placed in the Federal Code.

My purpose in this chapter is to provide compressed medical information from a scientific perspective to help us make wise political decisions ranging from what has been termed "an opioid crisis" to debate on the legalization of cannabis (marijuana) products.

You will discover with me that there are four federal issues that impact us the most: Social Security, Internal Revenue Service (IRS) tax collection, health policy and Illegal Immigration. The second issue, IRS, can be removed completely from our lives if we work at it through the Social Security process, except for paying income taxes on other income earned. This statement assumes that soon all Social Security taxes on earned entitlements are eliminated. That is one of the primary goals of mine and one of the salient points in Chapter 3 on Social Security.

There are so many political issues involving health of those in the Gray Zone. I will cover pain problems and solutions, Alzheimer's, care giving in institutions or at home, community resources, neglect, high costs of care and prescription drugs, the case of veterans and indigents, and finally health insurance including Medicaid. I have compressed a lot of information into this one chapter and encourage everyone to consult the sources I use and the vast numbers of articles and books pertaining to the subject.

One must be careful here to maintain an open mind. Many states have legalized marijuana, for example, based less on science and more on demand. In some sense it is like repealing Prohibition. We knew alcohol was bad for people when used excessively and addictively, that alcohol affected the liver and the mind, and that it is a public nuisance or even greater when a person under the influence of alcohol is involved in a car crash death via a DUI.

The politics of specific diseases is complex and not included in this book, except for one proviso here. If you donate to a cause, check how the money is being spent. I stopped giving a long time ago to the United Fund, because they were giving funds to cause with which I did not agree. Foundations that sound good still need further investigation by the Gray Zone on their expenditures and salary structure. If you agree with ALL their use of your dollars, by all means contribute.

Under the Trump Administration there is a new push to find ways to eradicate cancer in ten years. He made the announcement in the State of the Union Address, February 5, 2019. Gray Zone citizens have so many stakes in so many diseases and maladies including not just those affecting them, but those affecting family and friends that it is rare to have one health issue mentioned over another as a target for any period of time. Sometimes issues such as women's breast cancer catch the imagination of something like sports world so that the National Football League begins wearing pink shoes or paraphernalia to emphasize it. How that was selected as a disease of concentration was a marketing strategy to get more women interested in football. Looking at it objectively (you are going to say sure and you are a man) I have never understood by testicular and prostate cancer were not the beneficiaries. That, along with so many causes, is in the politics of various special interest groups and outside my purview.

Pain Problems and Solutions

Pain impacts the quality of life. On the surface this seems to be a no-brainer proposition with an expected conclusion. There is much more depth to the conclusion, but I doubt few would dispute the point unless they are sado-masochists. If you have ever experienced pain in your life, you understand this first point about impacting the quality of life. From causing temporary or permanent disabilities whether a migraine headache, or a broken bone, life just becomes more difficult. For the Gray Zone, you can double and triple that. Additionally, there is the psychological effect on us. Gray Zoner pain problems are magnified by other difficulties they may already have and lead to lethargy, depression, and some to suicide. The imagination assists in the magnification of the problem leading them to believe they have cancer or diabetes, or some other undiscovered lethal problem. We are all familiar with the person who we call a hypochondriac or person with a psychosomatic illness.[1]

There is little doubt that opioid use has increased along with cannabis (marijuana). The Internet is alive with a lot of debate about these issues. I recommend looking up both sides of the scientific perspective as it relates to painkillers of any kind and their beneficial versus harmful effects. I suspect reports of the salubrious effects of these solutions are prejudiced in their favor for various reasons. I am not one of those that accept the conspiracy theories of what has pejoratively been called "Big Pharma," for the pharmaceutical companies that produce the pills or the newly growing marijuana industry that is intent on replacing pain prescriptions. There clearly are rationales on every side of the argument from the scientific perspective that need to be investigated and taken seriously. On the other hand, I cannot accept a pill costing $1,000 in the United States and $4 in India as equitable. I will include that pill in the discussion. These are solutions that I suggest you research for yourself and consult with your doctor.

My concentration here is on finding the best path to resolving pain issues. You may have thought the percentage of senior citizens experiencing pain is much higher than surveys I found from two decades ago might suggest. In a Gallup survey in 1999 and a National Pain Foundation Telephone Poll of 2002, 55% of those over 65 (presumed by me from use of the term senior citizen) reported pain felt daily.[2] My original hypothesis was in the 75% range which included rheumatism, old injuries to joints and bones, deteriorating join structures, osteoporosis, and organ failures from kidneys to hearts and lungs. I suppose I could include pain from cuts and bruises to make it an omnibus of pain problems.

Take a trip with me through various pain management solutions from drug-free options to substance ingestion involving one of three likely candidates: narcotics, opioids or cannabis. That is almost like a time line of pain management resolution preferences, except for stem cell therapy being a new method of pain management making a circle out of the progression line. I am familiar with pain management, since my now departed wife had so many internal sources of pain, not the least was dealing with more past broken bones.

Drug-Free Pain Management

I was not surprised when I discovered that in a 2017 survey, 78% of Americans prefer nondrug ways to address their physical pain.[3] I thought the survey could have been higher, but it seems the survey covered the entire population and was not concentrated on senior citizens. Personally, I have experienced pain, but my tendency is to learn to ignore it if I know what the cause was of the pain. That worked for a long time with my right hip, until I decided to have it looked at by a doctor, since I was becoming less able to navigate on my feet. Sure enough, the hip joint socket cartilage was gone.

The National Pain Foundation sponsors the "National Pain Report." That is not just for the Gray Zone. They cover society. An overall figure of theirs on their website states that "Pain costs up to $635 billion in medical treatment and lost productivity."[4]

My now deceased wife was on opioids and suggested I use them, but I refused. Her pain was so prevalent from assorted bones broken by previous abusive husbands and her own athletic nature to the tune of 46 broken bones. In good conscience I understood her need for opioids and why her doctors continued to prescribe them. She also used the drug, Tramadol, which is a narcotic-like drug, but one of the older respected drugs for pain. In addition, she had pharmacy produced analgesic ointments made by a pharmacy in Conroe, Texas, and I had to buy Aspercreme for her as well to supplement the pharmacy remedy. In other words, she had a cornucopia of pain remedies and employed all of them.

Drug-free solutions traditionally include liniments and exterior applied analgesics, surgery, folk remedies and acupuncture. Add to that stem cell therapy that is already becoming the newest method of curing pain by regenerating organs and body parts, at least in the near future. Homeopathic medicines are relied upon by millions of

Americans and form the bridge between external and internal remedies. I have only to mention Chamomile Tea, Lavender, St. John's Wort, and other herbal solutions applied topically or ingested to make my point.

Homeopathic Remedies

Controlling homeopathic remedies is like trying to control gardening. Everybody seems to have one passed down from generation to generation like Aunt Millie's recipe for Elderberry wine. If they do not have such a remedy, their neighbors will make certain they do. Please understand that I do not make fun of homeopathic brews, just the ones like the original Kikapoo Joy Juice from the Lil Abner cartoon. Buy the way, there is a brand of Kikapoo Joy Juice® produced by Monarch Brands.

I will give you sales figures by 2018 that are the visible market for such products, but I estimate the hidden market products if monetized would double the figure to around a $1 billion industry in the United States. According to a report in Statista, the total visible sales figure is $437.3 million.[5] This number is lower than about ten years ago. Looking through various reports it was over $500 million. The present number is broken down into $174.4 million for cold and flu relief, $84.9 million for pain relief, $81.6 million for children's medicine, and $1.9 million for digestives.

I have a neutral position on homeopathic medicines, except it is dependent on the producer of the product for the quality and ensuring that it does not have other adverse effects such as allowing lead from a radiator to leach into the alcohol produced by a still. I point out that there is no guarantee unless you mix up the potion yourself from a recipe and make sure there is nothing contained in the recipe that is even more hazardous to the health, or contaminate the final product.

The Federal Trade Commission has reluctantly looked at homeopathic medicines on occasion and seems more inclined presently to get more directly involved. It will be interesting to see how this affects market production and revenue.

Salts, Liniments, and Rubs (Lanacane)

My dad was once a farmer and then a school custodian. He used to place his feet in Epsom Salt(s) to relieve foot pain. An article on PainScience.com is one of many I found on the Internet that says Epsom Salt(s) has no therapeutic power. According to the article:

Epsom salt (magnesium sulfate) in your bath is cheap and harmless and it makes the water feel "silkier," but it probably doesn't do anything else you hope it's doing. Contrary to popular belief, it probably has no significant benefits for most common kinds of aches and pains.... Topical delivery via creams is scientifically controversial, and absorption from baths is virtually unstudied: it may not work in a bath at all, or only modestly and erratically. For pain, the soothing heat of a nice bath is probably far more therapeutic than whatever magnesium might be absorbed. Bathing in a magnesium sulfate solution also has no other known medical benefits other than treating skin infections. Most theories you hear about how Epsom salt baths work are oversimplified and meaningless (for instance, nearly everyone says it is absorbed by osmosis, which is definitely wrong). The case for the healing powers of Epsom salt is mostly made by people selling the stuff, or recommending it as carelessly as an old wives' tale. If relatively dilute home salt baths were actually medicinal, then far more concentrated sources like The Dead Sea would have clear health effects, which they definitely do not.[6]

Like a lot of folk remedies, Epsom Salt or Salts, however you wish to call it, does nothing that rubbing the area and feeling better after placing the limbs in hot water alone will not do.

I remember the Watkins Liniment bottles from the 1940's. Liniment and a broad array of medications for topical application to the skin are topiceuticals. There is an extensive array of topical applications for everything from treating bronchitis like a mustard plaster, to pain relieving skin patches. Simply all of these work to some degree depending on the strength of the application and the nature of ache. For a description of the effects of these topiceuticals, I recommend referring to the article titled, "Liniment" found in <u>Science Direct</u>.[7]

Lanacane and Lidocane are topical rubs that have been found to relieve muscle pain. Lidocane has two additional effects and that is relieving itching and being antibacterial, which thus helps disinfect cuts.

NSAIDS and Related Pills

I probably should have used the generic aspirin, Tylenol, and Ibuprofen as the title here, since that is how most of us recognize it. These are most recognized as headache remedies, but they are also a universal pain medication that lasts for however long is specified on the box for the particular brand. The political problem is not with the pills, but with substitutes such as cannabis.

Narcotic Pain Management

Tobacco was used by American native tribes not just for signing treaties, but as a pain medication. We all understand the taxes levied on tobacco are there to supposedly be used to treat tobacco related health problems; however, I have my doubts those funds are used exclusively for that purposes, since they go into the general fund.

Opioid Pain Management

You do realize that opioids are derivatives of opium, don't you? Heroin is a powerful street drug along with Fentanyl which is derived from the poppy as well. Opioids are a type or subset of narcotic as they are defined. The primary medications that are opioid based are as follows:

- Codeine (only available in generic form)
- Fentanyl (Actiq, Duragesic, Fentora, Abstral, Onsolis)
- Hydrocodone (Hysingla, Zohydro ER)
- Hydrocodone/acetaminophen (Lorcet, Lortab, Norco, Vicodin)
- Hydromorphone (Dilaudid, Exalgo)
- Meperidine (Demerol)
- Methadone (Dolophine, Methadose)
- Morphine (Kadian, MS Contin, Morphabond)
- Oxycodone (OxyContin, Oxaydo)
- Oxycodone and acetaminophen (Percocet, Roxicet)
- Oxycodone and naloxone[8]

Many of these are recognizable from the morphine that is used in emergency medical treatments to the codeine that is used in cough medicines. Opioid drugs are the most prevalent form of serious pain killers. Oxycodone, Vicodin, Percocet and Demerol are also commonly prescribed drugs for senior citizens.

According to the National Institute of Drug Abuse, "All opioids are chemically related and interact with opioid receptors on nerve cells in the body and brain. Opioid pain relievers are generally safe when taken for a short time and as prescribed by a doctor, but because they produce euphoria in addition to pain relief, they can be misused (taken in a different way or in a larger quantity than prescribed, or taken without a doctor's prescription). Regular use—even as prescribed by a doctor—can lead to dependence and, when

In 2017, the Trump Administration addressed a crisis in opioid use declaring a national medical emergency and signing legislation to control more tightly through careful prescribing, take back programs, and by controlling illegal entry through ports, shipments and border crossings. An excellent presentation of this effort can be found on "Opioids.gov." The severity of the problem was highlighted on this website with the figure that 63,632 deaths were attributed to opioids in 2016, almost twice as many as deaths from auto accidents and one-third more than those attributable to breast cancer.[10]

Cannabis Pain Management

I know for a fact without conducting exhaustive research that the vast majority of the population will find a source they think makes a good argument on one side or the other of an issue and say, look what I found. Now I am in favor, or now I am against something. I see it every day in my social media inputs. My friends have not checked on who said something and why they said it. This is how fake news has made such an impact in our thinking the past decade. We are predisposed to give immediate approval to something that supports our preconceived notions or interests. This is particularly true on issues like going to Mexico to get cancer treatments, or reporting to others that marijuana can cure pain without deleterious side effects. They will then have an article or statement to back them up, but they do not go beyond step one. That is the step of unsubstantiated discovery.

I would say I am hazy on the effects of cannabis/marijuana use to Gray Zone citizens, but some of you would ask what I have been smoking. I simply have not sorted it all out myself at this point. I am one of those in the Gray Zone who has never tried marijuana or cannabis oil and am predisposed never to do so. My prejudices were well founded on it being possibly brain altering; leading to addiction through follow on drugs that purveyors might try to sell me thinking well if I had gone this far, why not more; and the fact that it is/was illegal throughout the United States.

One who has been trained to conduct research, such as myself, will go into the subject more deeply on both sides of a question and provide their sources for substantiation. I just mentioned that I was predisposed against the use of cannabis/marijuana. That is what a scientific researcher does to alert readers to potential bias. I also said I intend to keep an open mind, which is the trait of a scientific researcher. As you know, I also said in the first chapter that I intend not to make this an academic research paper. I said that I wanted to make our discussion more "folksy." I assure you I have read sufficiently and could have used fifty or more sources in each chapter, but I boiled them down to just a few endnote sources that you can read and then go on to conduct a more thorough search if you are so inclined and make up your own mind.

The place to begin our understanding of medical marijuana is with the U.S. Food and Drug Administration (US FDA) and valid scientific studies such as those conducted by the National Institute on Drug Abuse, a U.S. government funded institute.

The FDA has yet to approve the use of cannabis despite what the states have decided regarding the legalization of marijuana and its derivative oils. There are 113 compounds[11] found in the marijuana plant, some of which are used in other drugs as a cheaper source these days. The plant does contain two substances, cannabidiol (CBD) and tetrahydrocannabidiol (THC), which is the mind-altering drug that I call "The High Cloud." The first drug that uses one of the two key substance compounds cannabidiol (CBD), found in cannabis, however, was approved in 2018 as the prescription drug name,

Epidiolex, for rare severe cases of two types epilepsy in children.[11] Warning! Without my warning, some of you would go running off assuming the FDA approved the medical use of marijuana! That is not what they did.

An article in the <u>Denver Post</u> (June 25, 2018) included this provision, "FDA officials said the drug reduced seizures when combined with older epilepsy drugs. The FDA has previously approved synthetic versions of another cannabis ingredient for medical use, including severe weight loss in patients with HIV. Epidiolex is essentially a pharmaceutical-grade version CBD oil, which some parents already use to treat children with epilepsy. CBD is one of more than 100 chemicals found in marijuana. But it doesn't contain THC, the ingredient that gives marijuana its mind-altering effect. Physicians say it's important to have a consistent, government-regulated version."[12]

There is one recent research report on the use of CBD that should be a caution to everyone about this one compound, let alone THC, which I also dub the villain. "CBD…appears to increase pressure inside the eye of mice, suggesting the use of the substance in the treatment of glaucoma may actually worsen the condition."[13]

One of the primary US government institutes that receives and investigates relevant studies from throughout the world on marijuana use is the National Institute on Drug Abuse (NIDA). A letter from the Director, updated to June 2018, provide some insights on "possible effects" of marijuana on various aspects of health. Citing various studies there were two items that were of interest for our purposes under the subheading, "What are Marijuana's effects on other aspects of physical health?" The first effect was increased heart rate by "20 to 50 beats per minute or may even double in some cases. Taking other drugs with marijuana can amplify this effect."[14] The second effect was "Limited evidence suggests that a person's risk of heart attack during the first hour after smoking marijuana is nearly five times his or her usual risk."[14]

Those two risks alone are sufficient to issue cautionary warnings about the use of cannabis by those of us in the Gray Zone. Checking further into the "Letter" there were warnings that use for Alzheimer's patients may or may not help them and that psychiatric effects such as schizophrenia were associated with long term use. The question left for research is on starting as senior citizens and being close to one of those two difficulties with or without knowing about it.

To be perfectly frank, marijuana research has a long way to go; however, if there is a chance that it worsens glaucoma, and increases chances for mind disorders and deterioration of the brain, that is sufficient for me to come to my own conclusion.

Now that I have covered the scientific side, let's take a look at a particularly seductive Internet article placed there especially for seniors. First note that the source is not an objective one, but one prepared by "Harvest of Tempe" a marijuana marketing and selling organization in Arizona that has a direct stake in selling marijuana. The site was marked "Senior Directory," and the article was titled, "10 Things Seniors Need to Know about Medical Marijuana."[15] I present their feel-good article about marijuana use by seniors as one of many that organizations may use for their own political and sales purposes.

The article begins by suggesting that senior citizens grew up during the time when marijuana was illegal and thus there is a negative stigma attached to its use, thus seniors "may perhaps" be the most misinformed, but "might also be the age demographic that benefits most from this natural plant." The use of "may perhaps," "might be," and "natural plant" are already red flags to me. Belladonna is also a natural plant and you should know how poisonous that is. You make up your own mind. Here are the ten points they try to make:

1. "Marijuana is SAFER than many commonly prescribed medications." They make the point that the side effects of many prescription drugs are much worse, no one ever died from an overdose, and "The powerful anti-oxidant effect of marijuana can provide relief for many disorders including liver inflammation from Hepatitis C, lupus, irritable bowel syndrome, and many other serious medical conditions...."

2. "Marijuana is not addictive." As I mentioned that may or may not be the case depending on genetics among other things.

3. "Marijuana can reduce and possible replace many prescription medications." The point is then made that they can enhance opiate based painkillers effects.

4. "There are many different types, or "strains" of marijuana." The two major strains they mention are Sativa and Indica, which they claim have different properties.

5. "There are marijuana strains without 'the high.'" Harvest of Tempe says their "cultivators have developed and are currently producing potent CBD genetic strains that have minimal psychoactive effect." They carry liquid extracts that have no "high" at all.

6. "There are ways to use marijuana other than smoking it." Harvest of Tempe then provides a list of delivery methods from cookies and candies to butters and oils.

7. "Marijuana-infused ointments can be very effective in alleviating arthritis and neuropathy pain." It can be used for joint, muscle and back pain without the high.

8. "Marijuana does not lower your IQ or cause brain damage." They cite the fact "There is no documentation that marijuana reduces or 'kills brain cells.'" They add that Alzheimer's and Parkinson's patient studies "indicate" it may encourage "new neural pathways" and "stop degeneration of brain cells.'"

9. "Marijuana can help increase appetite." Then they cite a study published in the American Journal of Epidemiology that is can also lower body weight.

10. "The stigma around medical marijuana use is fading."[15]

I could go through each of these claims, some possibly relevant and some irrelevant. Again, I refer you to scientific studies and the major point of most of them that further study is needed on all aspects of marijuana use, the distinctions between young versus old using it, and that the FDA has not concluded there is definitive enough information from these studies to allow the plant and its compounds to be used other than for some extreme cases like epilepsy.

I do not trust the words of a company that wants to sound like they have real evidence on their side and manufacture additional relevant points, when that company is a new primary marketer and seller of cannabis products.

Alzheimer's Disease

According to a 2012 report by The Marist Poll of thousands of seniors, Alzheimer's is the most feared consequence of old age.[16] There are so many jokes about people in the Gray Zone, but I find most of them about forgetting distasteful. I know I am fortunate that I still have an active mind that does not forget things, but many of my friends were that way from teenage years. I do not expect them to perform much differently now. In my case it may be I am blessed genetically, since my father never forgot anything until his death at the age of 91 and my mother's mind was good until she died at the age of 100. Still the thought of Alzheimer's is my greatest fear in my aging. A neighbor asked me one time if I was having a "senior moment" when I was thinking about a question. I sharply retorted, "I do not have senior moments." Just the mention of it bugs me, but that is likely a visceral reaction to the distant fear that I may be harboring.

Facts on Alzheimer's:
1. Irreversible, progressive brain disorder.
2. Mostly first symptoms being in mid-60s
3. An estimated 5.5 million Americans may have some form.
4. Ranked as the sixth leading cause of death in the US, but as a cause of death for older people it may rank 3rd.[17]

The application of Gray Power in the case of Alzheimer's would likely have little effect; however, I do worry about some people in positions of authority such as a Supreme Court Justice at present who I believe operates only through her law clerks who put everything together for her.

In any event the disease receives a lot of attention and a lot of funding. Among the latest news on potential cures or at least preventive measures is the discovery by the Salk Institute of the neuroprotective and anti-inflammatory properties of a native California shrub, the Yerba Santa, or "Holy Herb" as it would be translated. Native devotees have brewed its leave to treat respiratory ailments, fever, headaches, "and mash it into a poultice for wounds, sore muscles and rheumatism.[18]

While the research is preliminary a potent molecule was identified in the lab called "sterubin" that was the most active component of the plant. It showed powerful effects on the brain cells of mice. Since that is as far as they have gotten, it will be a considerable time in the process of eventually becoming a drug, but there may be hope out there as with so many promising things like the stem cell therapy.[18] There is a drug already on the market touted as helping the brain that was found in a compound from jellyfish. That coupled with this discovery can go a long way toward eventual prevention of the inexorable deterioration process when diagnosed.

Care Giving/Remain in Home/Community Resources

As many of you have done, or perhaps all of you in the Gray Zone, I have experienced the need for care giving and caregivers for my own mother and father. The choice is either an institution or staying in their home when they can no longer care for themselves. The first choice completely turns over their care to a third party. The second choice of home care supplements the things they find difficult to do. Community resources go a long way toward helping the stay at home option. Meals on Wheels provide food delivery and cleanup. Visiting Angels can stay with them throughout the day or as scheduled to assist and clean the house. Churches are a primary community resource for assisting with elderly members or parishioners.

Often the problem is failure to ask or investigate the resources and that is where the children who are adults by this stage and may be entering or in the Gray Zone themselves come into make decisions. I have been an avid fan of the television series, "Everybody Loves Raymond," in which the subject of dad driving became an issue. Taking away the wheels is not an enviable, delightful prospect, since that means taking away independence. In decent sized cities, which I define as those over 50,000 population, transportation may be available to go to the grocery store and bank among other places by public transportation that stops at the home and assists them in embarking and disembarking from their vehicle.

Costs

Increasing costs of senior care facilities outpace Social Security COLA raises all by themselves. That may account for the strengthening reluctance to go to Camp Swami for the remainder of their lives. Genworth Financial conducts an annual survey of private nursing home rooms. "There are no cheap options for those without long-term coverage. Semi-private nursing home rooms cost $82,125 annually, a bill that has climbed nearly 17% over the past five years, according to Genworth."[19] For the record Genworth Financial sells long-term care coverage…. Private nursing home rooms now come with a median annual bill of $92,378…an increase of…nearly 19% since 2011.[19]

Let me call attention to the obvious. That is in five years with the rising cost of almost 4% per annum. That sum well outruns the COLA and I have not even added in rising prescriptions costs or supplemental insurance costs. Medicare does not cover long-term stays. Thus, seniors must first spend down their assets until they qualify for the government health insurance program. Let me point out another difficulty. Even in the lowest average cost per state of Missouri for a room in a semi-private nursing home, $2,537 per month/$30,438 is far above the average Social Security check of around $1,400. (See Chapter 3) The numbers just do not work without additional pension income and savings or equity to be sold.

Politically that is why I am fighting to mobilize the Gray Zone for the breaks in the tax code, dropping the Medicare tax, and other governmental program adjustments. Let me explain it another way. The funding is eventually going to come out of the same Trust Fund. Rather than an accounting exercise, it makes sense to me to put at least some of the available money at some point in the bank accounts of senior citizens.

IRS Tax Treatment

For those of you who are uncertain as to how the IRS treats nursing home expenses, "…nursing home expenses are allowable as medical expenses: I you or someone who was your spouse or dependent, either when the service was provided or when you paid the expense, is in a nursing home primarily for medical care, then the entire cost including meals and lodging is deductible as a medical expense. If the individual is in the home mainly for personal reasons, then only the cost of the actual medical care is deductible as a medical expense, not the cost of the meals and lodging."[20]

<u>Abuse and Neglect</u>

Abuse takes the forms of physical and mental abuse. Physical abuse is more than striking a person. It is anything that is deleterious to their health such as withholding prescription medicine, forcing them to do something against their will that could harm them, and keeping them in unhealthy or stressful conditions. Mental abuse is much more difficult to prove since there usually is no physical evidence.[21]

Abuse and neglect are part of the same continuum. In fact, one form of abuse is neglect. I employ the use of the term "neglect" advisedly, since there are many reasons for the neglect, some of which are at the wishes of the person in the Gray Zone. The real meaning of the term as a noun is a state or fact of being uncared for and as a verb meaning left alone or failing to care for properly. We all believe we know what neglect is and can identify it by looking at the condition or status of who or what is being neglected. Observations, however, may not tell the whole story. Someone may look bright and cheerful, have clean clothes, and seem to be in perfect health, yet underneath there is neglect of some kind by someone.

There are state agencies that may be contacted to report potential cases of abuse. These can be communicated by phone with paperwork to follow. Trained Counselors are there to answer the phones. I recommend, however, that this be used only in extreme cases that are discovered, since it may be easy to get someone in trouble when it is not deserved.

Veterans

On social media I continue to see slogans of veterans first and take care of veterans before illegal immigrants. For those of us in the Gray Zone, Veterans saved us in World War II, the Korean War, the Vietnam Conflict, in Iraq and in Afghanistan! The young generation is getting away from the protection of those who gave their lives, their limbs, and sometimes their families in order to set the world straight.

I understand that Veterans now have highly improved health care under the Trump Administration. In fact, he moved quickly to solve a number of problems plaguing VA for a long time. As NPR reported, here is a recorded interview of Quil Lawrence fact checking the President as interviewed by Robert Siegel, Host of <u>All Things Considered</u>:[22]

"ROBERT SIEGEL, HOST:
Among the many issues President Trump touched on in his speech to veterans today was naturally care for veterans and ongoing reforms at the VA. To hear about what is and what isn't happening at the VA, we're now joined by NPR's Quil Lawrence. And, Quil, how much has the president done for veterans since he took office?
QUIL LAWRENCE, BYLINE: Well, he has signed some important laws. Very recently he put through something that's called The Forever GI Bill, which extended GI Bill benefits to more people and allow them to use it for a longer amount of time. There's a VA Accountability Act which makes it easier to fire misbehaving VA officials. And Trump mentioned today some changes in the way VA clinics will operate.
(SOUNDBITE OF ARCHIVED RECORDING)
PRESIDENT DONALD TRUMP: We are publishing wait times online for every VA facility so you know what the wait is. We've

delivered same-day emergency mental health services at every VA medical center.

LAWRENCE: In fact, he signed another law on stage at the convention today which makes it faster and easier for vets to appeal their VA decision about disability ratings. Now, many of these ideas are bipartisan consensus ideas as they have been around for years. But now they're moving relatively fast through Congress to the president's pen.

SIEGEL: This is worth noting here. You're talking about Congress acting in a bipartisan fashion, sending legislation quickly to the president. He's signing it. This is the exception to the rule in Washington these days, Quil.

LAWRENCE: It's like a parallel universe or something (laughter). The - but vets' issues have always been less partisan. And now with Republicans controlling Congress and the White House, they sort of own the VA. So, some of the bashing of the VA, some of the political obstructionism has gone. Now, some critics, like the DNC, today said, well, Trump is just taking credit for things that have been already in the works for years. Now, this isn't unusual for a politician to do that. And Trump today at the American Legion did say that last year, he had promised them he would fix the VA.

(SOUNDBITE OF ARCHIVED RECORDING)

TRUMP: And you see what's been happening. Now you have a true reformer in Secretary David Shulkin. He has done an incredible job.

(APPLAUSE)

SIEGEL: Now, Quil, Secretary Shulkin may be a true reformer, but he's also a true holdover from the Obama administration - so not a radical change from the VA leadership. Has that been well-received?

LAWRENCE: Yes. I think the continuity has been appreciated. Shulkin spoke at the Legion today, too, and he got a great reception. I should say the VA still isn't fully staffed up. There are no nominees for the top three positions under Shulkin. But he, Shulkin, has been announcing big changes, including slaughtering some sacred cows.

He dropped the VA's long-suffering in-house electronic medical record. I know it sounds boring, but it's hugely important. It means that they'll be able to take electronic records from the Pentagon and send them straight over to the VA. He's opened up mental health care to veterans with other-than-honorable discharges. These people had figured high in the suicide epidemic. So, he is getting some stuff done.

SIEGEL: Now, the president and the VA secretary also mentioned today the continuation of the Veterans Choice Program which lets veterans get care outside the VA system. With things moving so relatively fast at the VA, what about the concern that this program could be a slow-moving privatization of veterans' health care?

LAWRENCE: No matter how many times they deny it, that keeps coming back. Vets Choice, as we've reported on, hasn't really been a poster child for private care. The program Veterans Choice allows certain veterans to get care outside the system. It's been problematic. Shulkin today was talking up plans to reform it. We're hoping to see something like that in the fall. But even so, at the end of his speech today, he still felt the need to say that he will never, ever privatize the VA. And that got a big applause from the audience at the American Legion.

SIEGEL: That's Quil Lawrence, who covers veterans' affairs for NPR News. Quil, thanks.

LAWRENCE: Thanks, Robert."[22]

The issue of giving anything to illegal aliens will be discussed in the next chapter.

Indigents

Indigents or homeless are difficult cases for health care. Estimates of the homeless always seem to hover between $450,000 and 500,000. For one thing they are reluctant to go to a hospital or doctor. For another, their conditions are usually less than clean. There are a good many programs serving meals with special concentrations around Thanksgiving, Christmas and Easter. Often the food they eat may be tainted or old coming out of trash containers behind restaurants. "Poor **health** can contribute to being **homeless**, and being **homeless** can lead to poor **health**. Limited access to **health** care can make it worse. That's why the **health** of **homeless** people in the United States is worse than that of the general population."[23] This quote from Medline.gov gives the dimensions of the problem. Most local jurisdictions have programs to attempt to ameliorate homelessness and get them into some type of permanent accommodation. Medline in fact suggests that is the place to start.

The main problems of the homeless concerning health issues are:

1. Mental health
2. Substance abuse
3. Bronchitis and pneumonia
4. General conditions of being outdoors
5. Wound and skin infections.

"Many homeless women are victims of domestic or sexual abuse. Homeless children have high rates of emotional and behavioral problems, often from having witnessed abuse."[23]

Now tell me for heaven's sake why you would want to accept 1,000,000 illegal immigrants without a home into our country every year, when we do not solve our own citizen problems? There is no sane argument for admittance/allowance of illegal aliens into our country.

Compassion be damned for illegals! Have compassion for our own citizens!

Pharmaceutical Companies and the Cost of Prescriptions

Personal story. At the end of 2017, my wife's prescription coverage hit a ceiling and the last two months of a couple of drugs she was using had to be paid out of pocket. I remember the cost being over $200 for a two month supply to get her into the new year of one of the drugs. Medicare at that point also would not cover it for some reason. I paid the cost at the pharmacy. But when I got home, she told me she would have found another way not to spend our precious dollars.

That was my real introduction to the costs of medication prescriptions.

She told me that if it were not for the National Kidney Foundation, she and her previous husband would have had to pay $15,000 a month for medications and dialysis. Then a friend of mine told me privately that she and her husband had to get a divorce so he could have his heart replacement paid.

These stories then were amplified in my mind by the surging costs of some types of insulin prescriptions headed by the exorbitant new prices of long acting insulin manufactured by Novo Nordisk whose biggest cash cow is Levemir, a long-acting insulin that went from $144.80 per vial in 2012 to $335.70 in January 2017. [24] Some of my social media friends were affected directly, so I paid attention to what was happening with medical drug prices in the United States. I remembered some things I learned in the past in one of my graduate studies seminars. First, I knew that the cost of development of specialized medicines had an exorbitant cost, some of which was caused by laboratory research, some by initial testing costs, and some by validation over five years.

Back to Novo Nordisk, the most recent villain. Prices of their long-lasting insulin had begun skyrocketing in 2016. The U.S. government and state governments began pressuring the pharmaceutical firm. President Trump was a leading critic at the federal level and states like Massachusetts began lawsuits against the firm, which is based in Denmark. "A Massachusetts law firm sued the company and two other pharma companies on behalf of patients, claiming that high insulin prices of hundreds of dollars a month forced diabetics to starve themselves to minimize their blood sugar while skimping on doses."[24]

How did Novo Nordisk fight back? Aggressive lobbying. Novo Nordisk through their Political Action Committee, spent $405,000 in campaign donations and other political outlays, which was "more than in 2016" an election.

"Novo Nordisk also spent $3.2 million lobbying Congress and Federal Agencies in 2017, its biggest-ever investment in directly influencing US policy makers....[24] Part of the expense was bringing 400 employees to contact lawmakers and staffs on Capitol Hill.[24]

Big Pharma companies "gave" $13.6 in political donations in 2016 and $12.1 million in 2017. Total lobbying expenses were more than $171 million in 2016. The concentration was on the power leaders of both political parties. Much of that had to do with negotiations and presentations over the revising of the Affordable Care Act.[24]

Analyzing costs of drug development from laboratory to government approval is undoubtedly costly and there are a great number of variables involved for each step. These vary from the cost of trials in poor countries to the five-year approval process in the United States.

Stages from conception to consumer:

1. Drug Discovery
2. Investigational New Drug (IND) FDA Application
3. Preclinical Drug Trials
4. Clinical Trials and Monitoring
5. Success or Failure
6. Approval

1. Drug discovery is rated by far as the most extensive step in the process; however, pharmaceutical companies volunteer the numbers and may use figures from one drug to cover losses on investigation into a number of other drugs simultaneously, as well as the trial costs of the drug itself, counting "capitalization" of the long period of ten or more years. Thus "companies often do not report whether a given figure includes the capitalized cost or comprises only out-of-pocket expenses, or both."[25] (Wikipedia) An analysis of drug development costs for 98 companies over a decade, average

cost per drug approved was $350 million, but companies that had multiple drugs approved of over a decade, the cost was as high $5.5 billion.[26]

2. The Investigational New Drug FDA Application would seem like a simple step which would be accomplished by simply providing notes and formulas; however, there is a back and forth agency/company dialogue that may result in tweaking over a period of time. There is a huge cost for the application that is between one and two million dollars. This figure comes from 2014.[27]

3. Preclinical Trials. Drug development and making decisions on the appropriate compound mix and size is relatively the most inexpensive testing period, since non-human subjects and working on animals from rats to monkeys occurs; however, the FDA has a mandated 3-phase clinical trial process that must include studies of side effects and effectiveness of the drug. A single phase of the preclinical trial can cost as much as $100 million or more.

4. Clinical Trials and Monitoring. Human testing is tricky. To reduce costs, companies prefer to test on patients in the underdeveloped world where there are no restrictions and mistakes can be buried. In my graduate class for the Global Management MBA one of my team members, Christina, was working for pharmaceutical company and her business of corroborating statistics took her to places like Zaire, Zimbabwe and South Africa.

5. Success or Failure. Given an average time of 12 years from the lab to the patient, about 10% make it to patient testing and about 1 drug in 98 complete the entire process and makes it to the pharmacy and the doctor's weapons arsenal. Obviously "profits" from one successful drug have to cover the costs of failed drugs. In my research I was struck by the AstraZeneca report that they spent an average of $11 Billion per successful drug![28] I suggest they stop spending and live off what they have already accomplished reducing pill costs.

Having detailed the extreme costs of completing a success drug obstacle course, one might be tempted to just throw up their hands and say, "I give up." If we want new drugs, we have to be prepared to pay the costs. Either we are able to pay for and take the drugs, find alternatives at lesser levels with some improvement to our health, or forego extending our lives. This is where politics comes into play and the seductive voice of the Socialists come calling on voters to get it all free, disregarding the fact that companies may stop right there and not engage in new drug processes. We have to decide ourselves if we want better drugs and new medical discoveries. That also means the government taking over pharmaceuticals and we know how that can lead to disaster.

That takes us to a discussion of Medicaid, Medical Insurance and the overall cost of health care in the United States. Much of the focus up to this point is on individuals paying prescription prices. Medicaid could save big bucks on the cost of the drugs they negotiate and purchase on behalf of Gray Zone patients. We are all familiar with the political debacle of the Affordable Care Act under the democratic administration with passage of a 2,000 plus page bill that those in Congress admitted they did not read and then mandating a new tax on the American people to either pay for a massive coverage insurance cost or pay a tax to the IRS that ran into thousands of dollars. In my opinion that mandate meant their defeat at the polls in 2016, since there was such a large segment of the population was hit with a bill they could not pay.

Medicaid, Medical Insurance, and the Cost of Health Care

The Trump Administration has focused the spotlight on inequitable payments by Americans for drugs compared to other countries and challenged the pharmaceutical industry for their lower prices in other countries compared to the

United States prices. The charge is that these companies are subsidizing foreign sold medications of the same drug with American prices, or are simply soaking the American public. He made a proposal in October 2018 "that Medicare pay for certain prescription drugs based on the prices paid in other advanced industrial countries — a huge change that could save money for the government and for millions of Medicare beneficiaries."[29] The way it would work is by establishing an "international pricing index" as a "benchmark" in deciding what pharmaceutical companies should be paid by the government. Under the Affordable Care Act provisions that are still in existence, the Center for Medicare and Medicaid Innovation was created and could be used to carry out the proposal.[29]

The New York Times cited a government study that said Medicare was paying 80% more that other advanced countries for the same medicines and the President was taking aim at "global free riding" forcing Americans to subsidize drug prices elsewhere."[29] The New York Times added that the Secretary of Health and Human Services, Alex Azar, stated "Medicare was found to be paying the highest price for 19 out of the 27 drugs studied." In only one case was Medicare paying less than the international average...." Furthermore, "As an example, Mr. Trump said: "One common cancer drug is nearly seven times as expensive for Medicare as it is for other countries. This is a highly used and very effective drug." The president was apparently referring to Treanda, a cancer treatment sold by Teva Pharmaceutical Industries."[29]

Hepatitis C Pill Cost Discrepancy

I know you have seen recent television ads announcing a pill that in 2 weeks can cure hepatitis-C. According to several news outlets, the drug costs $1,000 in the United States and only $4 in India! What gives? "The companies sponsor screening drives, hand out free test kits to hospitals and offer bulk discounts to entire villages. Sofosbuvir was cheap by most any standard when it hit the market in Punjab at $10 in March. Then the cost kept dropping, to as low as $4.29, and doctors predict it will continue to fall. That's in contrast to the situation in the U.S., where Gilead set off a firestorm in December 2013 by listing Sovaldi at $84,000 for a 12-week course regimen."[31]

According to Dr. Stephen Holt, "2019 will hopefully see a drop in high costs coupled with more accessibility and fewer denials from insurers."[31] He reported "that half of privately insured Hepatitis C patients were denied treatment between 2016 and 2017, and denials from public insurers were also high at 34% over the same period. The reason for the high denial rate and restriction of access is undoubtedly cost, with researchers also finding that health insurance providers were granting approvals only for "patients with evidence of advanced liver fibrosis and/or abstinence from alcohol or illicit drug use."[31]

Dr. Holt reviewed competing FDA-approved treatments and prices set for 2019 for one round of treatment which is usually for twelve weeks at 1 pill per day:

1. AbbVie's drug Mvyret: $26,400/1 round of treatment.
2. Merck's drug Zepatier: $54,600
3. Gilead's Epclusa and Harvoni cocktail: $74,760
4. Vosevi: $74,000
5. Daklinza: $63,000 + Sovalidi: $84,000 = $147,000
6. Harvoni: $94,000 for 12-24 weeks
7. Sovaldi: $84,000 for genotypes 1,2,3,4.
    With genotype #3 it also requires Daklinza = $147,000[31]

The cost of prescription drugs and the costs of medical care are clearly a hot topic in the political parties. The party that seizes the upper hand in this one will have a significant plank in the platform that could sway the election results heavily in their favor, especially as the Gray Zone voters get to know the candidates and their stances on the subject.

I purposely did not go into a discussion of insurance costs, since the political scene is still so confusing, as are the options, but it remains of high political interest as well.

Debatable Propositions for Health Issues

1. Pain prescriptions must use the best available source to sufficiently squelch the pain, but not contribute to pain pill addiction.

2. Marijuana must not be deployed country-wide and perhaps even rolled back in the states, since the studies are in conflict and have not resolved the problem.

3. Homeopathic medicines need greater attention through studies and may offer a less expensive future alternative. In the meantime, information should be distributed on their effects and efficacy along with side effects when used compare to other medications. That takes more government involvement.

4. It may take a political solution to solve the problem of excessive increases in care giving institutions.

5. Veterans care is a priority and must always be available at whatever cost as a priority.

6. Continued stem cell research is important to the future of controlling costs and perhaps someday getting rid of using organs and body parts from expensive sources.

7. We need to support all measures possible to reduce insurance payments for medications and medical procedures.

Chapter 6

ILLEGAL IMMIGRATION ISSUES AND COSTS

A nation that does not control its own territory and populace loses its sovereignty and control of its own destiny and becomes the colony of others and the world. ~Roy E. Peterson

Illegal immigration is the second greatest internal threat to our country regardless of the segment of the population; however, illegal immigration negatively affects those of us in the Gray Zone (50+) disproportionately. We all are direct or indirect victims whether it be illegal welfare payments, hospital cost increases to cover nonpaying illegals, education costs including adding classrooms and teachers, dangerous drug importation, sex trafficking of women and children, documented rape of innocent victims that involve our children and grandchildren, or murder of American citizens including couples and individuals in the Gray Zone. Then we get to subsidize them through the various welfare programs including illegal subsidies through Medicaid loopholes.

The greatest threat is "immigrants' brought to America from the Middle East. The third greatest threat is socialism.

In the 2018 midterm elections, Illegal Immigration was a hot button topic. This is illustrated in a Rasmussen Report national survey. "According to the latest Rasmussen Reports national survey, 72 percent of likely U.S. voters say that the issue of illegal immigration is important to their vote in the midterm elections this fall, with 42 percent saying it is "very important."[1]

Yes, I am still being objective! The far left asks how can I be, or how is that by your words? My answer is, consider the logic first and how we are all affected second.

Logic alone dictates a powerful defense on American borders. You may call it horse sense or common sense, but it adds up to the same thing. For decades, even centuries we felt secure with Canada to the north, oceans on either side of the continental United States, and relative control of our southern border with Mexico. What has changed the most is the nature of the southern border. The problem has been recognized for decades and several administrations, but both parties let it fester. The reason why it festered was businesses were reluctant to give up their cheap labor and migrant workers had become a normalized feature of picking crops in California's San Joaquin Valley among other things and places. The *bracero* program brought thousands of workers to the United States when labor was needed starting with World War II. That program did not envision invasion.

I have only to ask two questions:

1. Is America a country or a world province?

2. Are you IN FAVOR of a high crime rate caused by illegals, drugs continuing to flood our streets causing untold economic loss and citizen debilitation ending in early death, sex trafficking of women and children, exposure to third world diseases, wasting our resources on people who do not have the right to our free goods and services, the multibillion dollar cost of assistance programs, and further economic loss through remittances back to their home country, voter fraud, false Congressional representation, OR AGAINST?

Those are objective criteria for humanity and the preservation of any society. Now I hear the faint question, don't you have compassion for them? My answer is another question, don't you have compassion for Americans, for our elderly citizens, for our homeless, for our veterans, for our taxpayers, for the health and welfare of our own children?

Then I hear the strident voices that they just want to come to our country like our forefathers and mothers did. Now I am getting that feeling in the pit of my stomach that makes me angrily rise from where I am sitting and lambaste fools for equating those who come here to rape, rob, and ruin our society these days from those of our ancestors who came legally, who were processed properly, and who became law abiding citizens for the most part in our great melting pot. Some of the illegal immigrants could have made it here legally.

Only legally processed immigrants are acceptable. They are checked by visa issuing officers for their backgrounds with agency checks and must go through medical screening to be accepted. I know. I served as Visa Issuing Officer when the State Department Visa Issuing Officer in Vladivostok, Russia went on vacation. I was a diplomat with the US Department of

Commerce and had the additional duty of Visa Issuing Officer for the US Department of State as agreed, approved, and studied at US Foreign Service Institute in Washington, DC.

The illegal immigrants and those who were scraped up from the Middle East who bring their own flags, refuse to assimilate, attempt to have their law replace American law, struggle to upend our great Republic, and aggressively seek to even vote, when they do not deserve to have that privilege, do not deserve the right looting our treasuries (federal and state), preying upon our citizens, as if we were subjects beholden to them, while living off the largesse of our welfare system.

If you do not live on the border of Mexico in one of four states: California, Texas, New Mexico, and Arizona you do not understand the threat to ranchers and their families on a daily basis. Although you may not live on the border, the threat to you is as real as being there facing hordes by yourself. You just fail to see and understand the problem.

Recently I have seen letters posted on social media from the wives of ranchers on the border that they have been intimated by groups of illegal immigrants, that they were stealing from the ranch, and that neighbors had been murdered!

I am not assigning blame to one political party or another, but to both American political parties. There are laws on the books such as fining a business for employing illegal aliens, but how many cases have your heard that were brought against them? I thought so. Hardly any unless a political figure was involved.

Pick a number with a lower end range from $3.3 Billion to 15.6 Billion[2] and then a high number of say the number used in 2017 by the Federation for American Immigration Reform (FAIR) of $155 Billion.[3] Cato Institute suggested the bottom range leaving out a host of taxes and other associated costs as well as trying to add the cost of more Border Patrol, when it should be reduced. As analyst, Steven A. Camarota of

FAIR, wrote in an article on May 1, 2017, "Even Cato Agrees: A Border Wall Can Pay for Itself."[4]

Estimates of the high cost of illegal immigration are like attempting to discover the number of demons that can dance on the head of a pin. They are relevant only in the sense that there is an undisputed cost of some billions. If $15 Billion were put into building the wall, even Cato would have to admit in less than 5 years it would pay for itself. I believe the avalanche of articles detailing must higher costs.

Why did I suggest irrelevancy? Three reasons: 1.) None of them count the damages done by criminal activity. 2.) I refuse to believe there is a complete picture of the number of illegals in this country. 3.) Lost wages by American labor. They are irrelevant in that the greater arguments to cost are the damages done to Americans directly and indirectly through crime and incarceration.

When I lived in California, I was a Vice President for a company seeking to build apartments in Victorville. I visited other sites and the Project Managers and Construction Supervisors said they employed illegals to cut the costs of manpower on construction jobs. I observed numerous groups of them working on the projects I visited and they were pointed out to me. I often was on a road connecting Interstate-5 with Interstate-15. At a juncture half way to Oceanside, I sometimes stopped for gas and a sandwich at McDonalds. Depending on the time of day there were upwards of 50 apparent illegal immigrants waiting to be picked up by someone for a day of work. I know they were illegal from having to talk to some looking for work and someone acting as a poor interpreter for them. I really hated to stop after a while, because they were becoming more aggressive, virtually blocking my car. They also made themselves scarce one day when a group of Californians appeared in pickup trucks with signs against illegal immigrants.

The Cato Institute is on the small end of the estimates and FAIR is on the large end. According to one article: "Cato Flubs Illegal Immigrant Numbers When Criticizing President Trump. This suggests that Cato underestimated the number of illegal immigrants by a significant amount even though they inappropriately claim 'we likely overestimate the number of illegal immigrants who are incarcerated." "Regardless of the estimates, the actual numbers do not add up.'"[5]

Sovereignty

Sovereignty is the right to govern a territorial area and populace within those borders without any interference whatsoever from outside sources or bodies. That is my slightly reworked definition from dictionary sources. Sovereignty is the keystone in the arch for a national government to even exist. I used to smile a little at graphics that had Native Americans saying they had open border and look what happened to them. I no longer even smile, since there is a new strain of criminal element in our country that does not want borders, border watchers, or border passage so they are free to commit crime, deal drugs, and engage in unfettered sex trafficking.

The Gray Zone citizens not only want borders, but needs them to begin feeling safer once again. Illegal immigrants are like the boogeyman in the room of a children who fears monsters. In this case some really are monsters. There is no choice other than to build walls, fences, obstacles, or anything else we can build to secure our people, not just in the Gray Zone, but our future citizens.

Illegals and "Rights"

Let us be very clear up front. Illegals have no rights, not to life, liberty, or the pursuit of happiness in the United States.

There are judges and juries that have been convened in trials against ranchers in Arizona and other states in which illegals have sued ranchers for intimidation, capture, and causing fear. Those judges should have dismissed the suit outright.

Legal rights are accorded guests in the United States like tourists, green card holders, and others with visas of various kinds, but do these judges not understand basic legal principles? First, they have no "standing." They are illegally here for goodness sakes! By the way that is the strongest curse words I ever use.

Crime

Remember my thesis in the beginning that if even one dollar is lost that is too much? The same applies in spades here. If even one crime is committed by an illegal, that is too much. It could have and should have been prevented. Any reasonable person would conclude that the billions of dollars lost and the threat manifested in crime in the United States because of illegal entrants is worth putting up a gargantuan well-protected wall. Apparently. we have people in Congress that either do not possess the good sense we are given, or are profiting personally in some way like accommodating drug dealers, using illegals for their own cheap labor reasons in homes or businesses, or receiving political contributions who thus favor maintaining a porous border. Then there are those who wish to give the world a vote in our elections! We must cull these people from the rolls of Congress!

There is an excellent study on all prisoners who entered the State of Arizona prison system from January 1985 through the end of June 2017 that separates no-U.S. citizens by whether or not they are illegal immigrants, or legal residents. Again, in dealing with illegal immigrants, we are dealing only with the tip of the iceberg that can be seen, quantified and assessed.

The numbers of crimes and the types of violent crimes they have committed are staggering.

From the report abstract, "Undocumented immigrants are at least 142% more likely to be convicted of a crime than other Arizonans. They also tend to commit more serious crimes and serve 10.5% longer sentences, more likely to be classified as dangerous, and 45% more likely to be gang members than U.S. citizens. Yet, there are several reasons that these numbers are likely to underestimate the share of crime committed by undocumented immigrants. There are dramatic differences in the criminal histories of convicts who are U.S. citizens and those who are undocumented immigrants. While undocumented immigrants from 15 to 35 years of age make up slightly over 2 percent of the Arizona population, they make up almost 8% of the prison population. Even after adjusting for the fact that young people commit crime at higher rates, young undocumented immigrants commit crime at twice the rate of young U.S. citizens. These undocumented immigrants also tend to commit more serious crimes."[6]

Chilling numbers are reflected here that the Gray Zone finds avoidable, reprehensible, and dereliction of the duty of our government to protect us, not to mention the personal cost, personal loss of our citizens, and fear that accompanies it. The study went on to make a scary extrapolation, "If undocumented immigrants committed crime nationally as they do in Arizona, in 2016 they would have been responsible for over 1,000 more murders, 5,200 rapes, 8,900 robberies, 25,300 aggravated assaults, and 26,900 burglaries.[6]

Do you need more evidence of the wholesale infliction of pain and suffering that unconscionably goes on under our very noses? Then I refer you to an earlier study by the Government Accountability Office (GAO) that was tasked to arrive at some numbers of illegal crimes in this country by type of offense committed. The figures given in the table show the numbers of illegal alien crimes for the period 2005 to 2010.[7]

Table 6-1: Criminal Alien Offenses by Category (2005-10)[7] and (2011-2016)[8]

Arrest Offense	Federal# 2005-10	Federal# 2011-2016	State# 2011-2016
Immigration	529,859	874,400	1,226,000
Drugs	504,043	336,600	761,200
Traffic	404,788	204,400	852,000
Assault	213,047	108,400	397,000
Larceny/Theft	125,322	70,300	276,700
Fraud, forgery, and counterfeiting	120,810	62,300	200,100
Obstruction of Justice	252,899	141,300	665,000
Burglary	115,045	44,900	175,000
Weapons violations	94,492	44,500	124,700
Motor Vehicle Theft	81,710	19,500	90,800
Sex Offenses	69,929	13,500	120,300
Disorderly Conduct	52,384	12,300	90,800
Stolen Property	49,126	14,300	75,500
Property Damage	42,609	17,500	x
Robbery	42,609	13,500	54,700
Homicide	25,064	6,000	x
Kidnappings	x	5,000	x
Arson	2,005	400	x
Terrorism	x	400	x
Other	151,138	74,200	257,000
Total	**2,891,668**	**2,016,400**	**5,402,900**

The conclusion of the first study is: "Illegals and noncitizens make up 3% and 8% of the population respectively, but commit at least 22% to 37% of the murders. Illegals likely commit **murder** at around 10 times the rate of all US inhabitants.... Around 6,000 people are killed by illegal aliens, almost all Latinos, every single year! "[7]

Notice the total of illegal immigrants incarcerated for both federal and state is 7,419,300! The GAO report in 2018 noted 208,800 criminal aliens were in state and federal prisons at an annual cost to taxpayers of $1.42 Billion down a little from the $1.56 Billion from the previous report.[8]

For our purposes as members of the Gray Zone, the numbers are illustrative and anecdotal. I use them simply to provide the scope of the enormity of the problem. I have seen challenges and counterchallenges to the statistical methods used by everybody with claims and counterclaims and I frankly do not care. What do people not get about an enormous problem? Logic and common sense tell us the Gray Zone is heavily affected, as is every other American citizen.

Illegal Employment Practices of American Companies

American companies are forbidden to hire illegal immigrants, yet they do. When they are caught the fines can be stringent. I will present just one case brought by The United States Attorney's Office for the Eastern District of Tennessee:

"On September 12, 2018, James Brantley, 61, of Bean Station, Tennessee, pleaded guilty before the Honorable J. Ronnie Greer, U.S. District Judge, to tax fraud, wire fraud, and employment of unauthorized illegal aliens. Brantley is the owner of Southeastern Provision, LLC (Southeastern Provision), a slaughterhouse and meatpacking plant located in Bean Station, Tennessee.

Brantley faces up to five years in prison, a $250,000 fine, and three years of supervised release for the tax counts. He faces a maximum of 20 years in prison, a $250,000 fine, and three years of *supervised release on the wire fraud charge. Finally, he faces up to six months in prison and a fine of not more than $3,000 per unauthorized alien on the employment of unauthorized alien charge. Brantley also agreed to pay restitution to the United States government in the total amount of $1,423,588 on or before the date of his sentencing. Sentencing has been set for 1:30 p.m., February 4, 2019, in U.S. District Court.....According to the plea agreement, beginning in 1988 and continuing through April 2018, Brantley knowingly hired, or caused others employed by him to hire, unauthorized aliens to work as employees at Southeastern Provision. The unauthorized aliens were knowingly hired to reduce Brantley and Southeastern Provision's FICA tax obligations, unemployment insurance premiums, unemployment tax obligations, and workers' compensation insurance premiums."*[9]

The federal search warrant that was executed in April 2018, stated *"agents discovered at least 104 unauthorized aliens employed there. Evidence showed that Brantley had previously reported to the Internal Revenue Service (IRS) that he had only 44 wage-earning employees. Further investigation revealed that he paid the unauthorized aliens in cash at a rate of $8-$10 per hour. The employees were also often asked to work overtime at their standard rate of pay, rather than the 'time and a half' required by the Fair Labor Standards Act for overtime work."*[9]

I could provide a comprehensive litany of lessons about getting caught using illegal immigrants; however, I believe one story is sufficient for this book. If I added more, I would finally write my doctoral dissertation. The story though in the case described covers so many angles: why businesses hire illegals, why they pay "under the table and simultaneously cook their own books just like the illegal still owners used to do" (which accounts for the IRS working with ICE on the raid). I contend the fine of only $3,000 per illegal immigrant by itself would have really been worth it to the business, which is why more charges were levied including wire fraud. The raid included the IRS, ICE and Tennessee Highway Patrol.

You will find numerous studies, papers and articles by pro-immigration organizations such as those filing papers in this case defending not only the illegal immigrants, but filing suit against those that conducted the raid! *"The suit was filed in federal court in Knoxville by the National Immigration Law Center, the Southern Poverty Law Center, and the law firm of Sherrard, Roe, Voigt and Harbison...."*[10] Thus there were two public advocacy groups and a law firm specializing in assisting illegal aliens in illegal immigrant cases.

I find it difficult to believe that anything could be filed again given the fact illegals have no standing in State or Federal Courts, but have been granted "illegal" access. Whatever happened to the legal determination of "standing?" That tells you when a legal system has gone corrupt.

Diseases

Feel good stories are about Doctors without Borders going to Central America and treating tropical diseases and diseases that the United States once conquered like bubonic plague, chicken pox, measles, mumps, tuberculosis, scarlet fever and whooping cough. Suddenly these diseases are reappearing in the last few years and the cause is illegal immigrants. That is because legal immigrants get checked and get vaccinated before coming to the U.S.

I am incredulous at the numbers of illegals who bring long past diseases conquered in the United States with them and begin infections nationwide. I am also incredulous that public health agencies like the CDC have not been tasked to come up with comprehensive statistics and tables concerning these diseases and from where they are coming. I had to rely on various sources for some of the data.

The first thing I learned is that states like California are warned by the political establishment there to forego reporting on the subject. The second thing I learned is that horrific diseases are brought here by their human vectors at an alarming rate and infecting our country when we had public health control in the past. They are truly a chaotic caravan of a vast array of diseases. The third thing I learned is that organizations that are pro-immigration have produced fake news promulgating the fact that these diseases are good for us to improve our health (somehow), that there are a few, and that we should just deal with it.

Wrong! Diseases are the bane and fear of the elderly. Those of us in the Gray Zone once felt comfortable that a flu shot annually and pneumonia shot would solve any disease transmission problem. We have lost our confidence now in public health and in politicians that struggle against the real facts of the situation.

Infections on an unprecedented magnitude are coming to America with illegal immigrants. We contact them in retail stores, businesses, construction sites, and restaurants. Our school age grandchildren and police forces come in contact on a daily basis, let along the poor Border Patrol agents and other law enforcement authorities.

First, I will detail a report in <u>The Dark Side of Illegal Immigration</u> describing various diseases.[11] Don't anyone disparage this report, since there are a variety of public sources that can be found on each case. The information is dated though, so guess how much has transpired in a decade. Then I will incorporate material from 2015-2016 on duplicate diseases. Here are the major diseases in the earlier report:

<u>**Dark Side Listings:**</u>

1. Malaria. Malaria was eradicated from the USA in the 1940's. Recent outbreaks were reported "in Southern California, New Jersey, New York City and Houston, and, "Malaria tainted blood has been discovered in the blood supply."[11]

2. Dengue Fever. Previously unknown in the U.S. "Dengue outbreaks have now occurred in the United States.

3. Leprosy (Now called Hansen's Disease). "In the 40 years prior to 2002, there were only 900 total cases…in the US. In the following three years there have been 9,000 cases and most were illegal aliens." The Breitbart article referred to an article by Dr. William Levies, Head of New York Hansen's Disease, title "Leprosy in America: New Cause for Concern," who said New York is endemic now, and nobody's noticed. Likewise, Dr, Terry Williams in Houston, who runs a clinic serving leprosy patients from across South Texas said the bulk of cases were immigrants.

4. Tuberculosis. "In an article in the Journal of the American Medical Assn., Dr. Reuben Granich, a lead investigator for the CDC commented on MDR-TB: "Evidence of it has surfaced in 38 of 61 California health jurisdictions, and it could 'threaten the efficacy of TB control efforts,' Granich said. The infected were said to be four times as likely to die from the disease and twice as likely to transmit the disease to others … Reluctant to label the infected as 'illegal' or even 'undocumented' aliens, the report notes that of the 407 known cases of MDR-TB, 84% were 'foreign-born' patients, mainly from Mexico and the Philippines who'd been in the U.S. less than five years."[11] [TB active/communicable cases tripled percentage wise for foreign born residents in the U.S. from 22 percent in 1986 to 66% of the active cases of 9.563. There were only 3,200 cases in 2015 of Native Americans and 6,300 reported of foreign-born cases mostly Mexico and the Philippines. Furthermore, the spread is all over the U.S. As reported in Breitbart News: "In the past five years, 21 in Louisiana, 10 in Colorado, 4 in Indiana, 11 in Florida, and 9 in one county of Kentucky. Latent cases were 26% in Indiana, 22% in Minnesota, 15% in Texas, and 12% in California."][12]

5. Chagas Disease (Trypanosomiasis). This disease is endemic to South and Central America through a bug that bites people. "It was unknown in the United States until fairly recently. It is now (2006) estimated that between 100,000 and 500,000 people in the US have Chagas Disease. Who is infect? Mostly illegal aliens."

6. HIV. "The number of illegal Mexican and Central American immigrants with HIV or AIDS is unknown, mostly because researchers rarely ask about immigration status. However, it is known that the rate of HIV infection among Latino women in California is about twice the rate of white women. At one free California health clinic, all of the women have HIV or AIDS. Most are Mexican or Central American 'immigrants.'"[11]

CDC and Breitbart Report:[12]

1. Measles: The CDC reported a record number of cases for the past 40 years when in 2014 the U.S. had 667 cases from 27 states reported to the CDC National Center for Immunization and Respiratory Diseases (NCIRD). It was documented measles had been eliminated in the U.S. by 2000. In 2019 we can watch on the daily news discussions of the need and/or resistance to getting vaccinations. Cases over the past four years were documented in Arizona, California, Georgia, Hawaii, Illinois, Massachusetts, Minnesota and DC. Then in 2016 one case was in a mosque in Memphis.

2. Pertusis (Whooping Cough): In 1926, over 200,000 had whooping cough in the US. In 1976, it had been reduced through vaccinations to 1,010. It crept back with gradual increases in illegal immigrants to over 4,000 in 1986. In 2014 reported cases grew from 1,010 in 1976, to 32,971 cases. There is no doubt the cause is immigrants either those hoisted from the Middle East or those illegals flowing across our Southern Border.

3. Other: Add mumps to the mix along with a host of other diseases including intestinal parasites, scabies, diphtheria, flesh eating bacteria and parasites, and Ebola (mainly from the African Continent).

Judicial Watch 2019:

"Weeks after mainstream media outlets reported that illegal immigrants don't bring disease into the United States, the Border Patrol reveals that it is getting slammed daily with dozens of illegal immigrants carrying "serious illnesses." This includes tuberculosis, influenza and pneumonia. In fact, a Guatemalan migrant who died in U.S. custody on Christmas Eve had Influenza B, a virus that causes respiratory infections. Federal agents are referring 50 illegal immigrants a day for urgent medical care, according to figures obtained by Washington D.C.'s **conservative newspaper**. Authorities say "it's unlike anything they've ever seen before." Many of the migrants have tuberculosis, parasites or the flue, the feds confirm. There are also lots of pregnant women about to give birth. The article quotes Customs and Border Protection (CBP) Commissioner Kevin McAleenan saying that most of the illegal immigrants were sick when they arrived at the U.S. border. "Many were ill before they departed their homes," McAleenan said. "We're talking about cases of pneumonia, tuberculosis, parasites. These are not things that developed urgently in a matter of days."[12]

"...the Coast Guard has been deployed to help, sending medical teams to Border Patrol sectors getting bombarded with sick migrants. They include Yuma and Tucson, Arizona as well as the Rio Grande Valley."[12]

"The biased coverage marked a great example of the mainstream media **distorting information** to promote a liberal agenda."[12]

"Judicial Watch has interviewed medical experts that confirm illegal immigrants do indeed pose a serious public health threat to the U.S. by bringing dangerous diseases into the country. This includes tuberculosis, dengue and Chikungunya. After returning from covering the Central American caravan along the Guatemala-Honduras border, Judicial Watch spoke with a prominent physician in a border state who **warned** that the migrants will undoubtedly bring infectious diseases into the U.S. Among them are extremely drug resistant strands of tuberculosis and mosquito-borne diseases such as dengue and chikungunya that are widespread in the region."[12]

"Years ago, when Barack Obama let tens of thousands of illegal immigrant minors into the country, health experts warned about the serious hazards to the American public. Most of the Unaccompanied Alien Children (UAC) came from Central America, like the current caravan, and they crossed into the U.S. through Mexico, in the same way that the caravan expects to. Swine flu, dengue fever and Ebola were among the diseases that the hordes of UACs brought with them, according to lawmakers and medical experts interviewed by Judicial Watch during the influx. At the time, a U.S. Congressman, who is also a medical doctor, **told Judicial Watch** about the danger to the American public as well as the Border Patrol agents forced to care for the UACs. The former lawmaker, Phil Gingrey, referred to it as a "severe and dangerous" crisis because the Central American youths were importing infectious diseases considered to be largely eradicated in this country. Many migrants lack basic vaccinations such as those to prevent chicken pox or measles, leaving America's young children and the elderly particularly susceptible, Gingrey pointed out then. To handle the escalating health crisis the CDC activated an Emergency Operations Center (EOC) that largely operated in secrecy."[12]

High Cost of Illegal Immigrants

Any cost is too much! Billions are catastrophe!

Estimates of the high cost of illegal immigration are like attempting to discover the number of demons that can dance on the head of a pin. FAIR estimates the number of illegal immigrants at about 12.5 million[13] while the CATO Institute estimates a million less.[13] I have the gall and the right to suggest that either estimate is half the number. How do you quantify the hidden numbers in our country? The answer is you can only quantify the visible part. The visible part is somewhere in the billions of costs for federal and state governments. Is that not enough to call a halt to the waste or resources and blocking out further erosion of our economy? I believe it is!

When I observe an evil that is becoming pervasive, my first tactic is to go to an extreme and ask the question, is that worth it? Take religion as an example. Would you approve of a cult that sacrificed women and children on a public altar and allow it to operate in the United States. Unfortunately, there seems to be a growing number of far-left people in our country who might accept such a cult these days and most of them are on the far-left wing of the Democratic Party. Now let me tell you I am thinking of the Aztecs and their religious cult. Where are you politically now?

Similarly, I categorically state that even the loss of one dollar of taxpayer funds is too much and must be stopped at whatever the cost when coupled with the social ills that come with the problem.

Illegal Immigrant Welfare

I found a rather dated source of information on welfare use from 2011 by the Center for Immigration Studies. Although it is eight years old, it provides an excellent insight and one can multiply by whatever factor they want to for a 2019 figure.

Unsurprisingly, Census Bureau data collected by a

nonpartisan Washington, DC group reveals most U.S. families headed by illegal immigrants use taxpayer-funded welfare programs on their American-born anchor babies at consistently higher rates than natives.[14] "States where immigrant households with children have highest welfare rates of use are Arizona (62%), Texas, California and New York (61% each) and Pennsylvania (59%).[15]

The study focused on eight major welfare programs that cost the government $517 billion the year they were examined. They include Supplemental Security Income (SSI) for the disabled, Temporary Assistance to Needy Families (TANF), a nutritional program known as Women, Infants and Children (WIC), food stamps, free/reduced school lunch, public housing and health insurance for the poor (Medicaid). Food assistance and Medicaid are the programs most commonly used by illegal immigrants, mainly on behalf of their American-born children who get automatic citizenship. Legal immigrant households take advantage of every available welfare program, according to the study, which attributes it to low education level and resulting low income.[15]

The highest rates of welfare recipients come from the Dominican Republic (82%), Mexico and Guatemala (75% each) and Ecuador (70%). Welfare use is high for both new arrivals and established residents.[15]

Medicaid

Although illegal immigrants are disqualified from receiving Medicaid benefits, they do cost American taxpayers $18.5 Billion annually. Chris Conover writing in Forbes stated "All told, Americans cross-subsidize health care for unauthorized immigrants to the tune of $18.5 billion a year. Of this total, federal taxpayers provided $11.2 billion in subsidized care to unauthorized immigrants in 2016."[6] That is one of the reasons the Social Security system is increasingly becoming insolvent as the years go along. This constitutes stealing from those of us who paid into the system and are paying now."[1]

As always once a fund has been "pierced," to use a legal term, the losses continue to grow. "The Center for Immigration Studies (CIS) found that the percentage of new immigrants on Medicaid grew from six percent in 2007 to 17 percent in 2017 – an increase of 11 percentage points. The percentage of Americans on Medicaid also slightly increased during the same time period, by nine percent."[1] Furthermore, "The average immigrant household consumes 33 percent more cash welfare, 57 percent more food assistance, and 44 percent more Medicaid dollars than the average native household,"[1]

Loopholes

1. **Medicaid and Medicare Subsidies**. If this is illegal, how does this get siphoned and why has it not been cut off? The regulations are strict even in the Affordable Care Act, but loopholes exist, such as an indirect receipt of $2.8 Billion states Medicaid programs and "through federal taxes totaling at least $4.6 Billion."[1] According to a report from the Henry J. Kaiser Family Foundation, the states of New York, Washington, Illinois, Massachusetts, California plus the District of Columbia "all provide state-only Medicaid benefits to illegal immigrants."[1]

2. **Community Health Centers.** Federal taxes indirectly fund these centers.

3. **Hospitals and Other Health Centers**. Many of these facilities are tax exempt. "Federal law requires that state Medicaid programs make Disproportionate Share Hospital (DSH) payments to qualifying hospitals that care for a large number of Medicaid and uninsured individuals. Because these hospitals are not restricted from using uncompensated care funds on illegal immigrants, the DSH Medicare and Medicaid

payments they receive indirectly fund aggregate uncompensated care losses from illegal immigrants."[1]

4. <u>Employer Tax Exclusions</u>.

Table 6-2

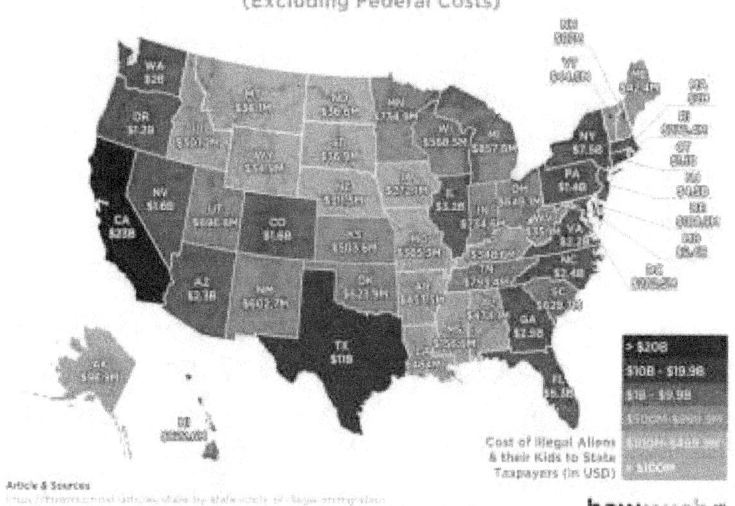

Source: https://www.judicialwatch.org/blog/2011/04/most-illegal-immigrant-families-collect-welfare/

Remittances

Remittances to foreign countries is a major loss of revenue that has been equated to a tax on America by other countries.[16] There is a lot of vitriol on the subject of remittances from one side believing it helps relatives in poor countries, helps the poor countries themselves and is worth the chance of them falling into the hands of drug cartels. The other side contends that is money that should be kept in the United States because it counts against our currency strength, that there are better ways to help poor countries with aid programs already in place and that it lines pockets in the long run of either Carlos Slim (the richest Mexican we know) or drug cartels.[17]

The top country receiving American dollars on an annual basis is Mexico followed by other Central American Countries. The problem is a lot of this money is also going to Drug Cartels. In 2015, Mexico received $24.4 Billion alone representing approximately 2% of the nations' economy. Remittances in 2015 surpassed oil exports as a revenue earner for Mexico for the first time in country history.[17]

I like the metaphor of one article titled, "Finding the Right Ballpark."[17] That is because no one has the "right bat" to play the game, if I may be permitted to extend the metaphor. "Reasonable assumptions" have to be made from a "reasonable set of data." If you have been reading this book and understand the way I think, the enormity of the situation is already attested to by the fact that the "ballgames" are played at high stakes. Quibbling over methodology is better left to the analysts who present their assumptions and data and then defend it against all comers.

As he various articles admit, there is no precise data on how much is remitted annually. We know from all of them that it is in the billions. Like I say, that is all I need to know for the figure that is finally used as long as the method of deriving the data is presented. You are going to ask though why we do not know.

1. The number of illegal aliens residing in the U.S. is less than precise by millions.

2. "The term remittance itself is ambiguous: should we include money stuffed in a birthday card?"[17]

3. We cannot track every dollar.

4. We are uncertain of who are the actual recipients. Do they wind up with the intended relatives, or do they get "taxed" on the way by gangs?

5. Are the remittances from first-generation legal immigrants or illegal aliens?

Finding the closest correct methodology involves critical thinking and then make assumptions like percent of remittance likely to be from each source. Dividing up the money into percentages by groups with assumptions about sending equal or unequal amounts of earnings is tricky, but the only way to arrive at a "reasonable" estimate.

According to a report by Pew Research regarding 2016 remittances to other countries, the outflow from the United States was $138.2 Billion.[18] Pew Research further showed the significance of the payments to some countries using El Salvador as one of the countries with the greatest dependency on the United State remittances. I just mentioned that for Mexico in 2015, it was estimated at around 2% of GDP, but for El Salvador, remittances from abroad were 17.1% of the GDP in 2016, of which 90% came from the estimated 200,000 living in the United States.

In making the case from a conservative standpoint, Spencer P. Morrison began his methodology with the closest accepted facts that there are 40 million first-generation immigrants and "(at least)" 11.1 million illegal aliens for a total just over 51 million.[18]

As I have suggested the illegal immigrant figure is far below the actual numbers that I believe are here. The analysis by Morrison presented a "recent study from Yale University" that there are at least 22.8 million illegals residing in the United States.[17] For the methodology Morrison then went with the 11.1 million as being the one most acceptable to all parties. Like I said, it should not matter to us, since the problem is like an elephant—it is enormous and right in front of us. We can see it unless we are blind. Morrison came up will $30 billion likely remitted by illegals and likened it to the entire annual Gross Domestic Product of Vermont.[17] Of course he slams the liberal Cato Institute for "routinely arguing in favor of open borders and for their repeated failure to grasp the significant of the losses to our own economy, in which Economists of every stripe tell us the turnover of money in our own economy has a multiplier effect and that investment is lost. That loss then actually corresponds to $300 million to $600 million lost to the United States given a multiplier effect either of 10:1 or up to 20:1. (I added the multiplier effect so you could understand the significance of the loss. (I minored in Economics, by the way). Remember this is without using the Yale figures for estimated number of illegals hidden away in our interior.

For the record, according to a World Bank Report, migrants both legal and illegal forwarded $53.4 Million in remittances to Mexico and Central America in 2018.[19] Remittances to Mexico alone reached $33.7 Billion in 2018, which was up by 21% over the 2016 figure of $27.8 Billion, and $19.7 Billion to the rest of central America, which also was up from $15.8 Billion in 2016.[19] According to Breitbart, GOP legislators suggested a tax be placed on sending remittances. He adds, "The money sent back from the United States to Central America includes many migrants' payments to the cartels who traffic them into the U.S. economy. The trafficking debts can start at $5,000 per head."[20]

There are more questions to be asked about remittances, although the size of the total added to costs associated with taking care of illegal aliens brings the total to at least $200 Billion annually. Point made! Enough said!

Voter Fraud

The laughable part of the investigation into voter fraud is that the biggest fraud is now perpetrated by illegal aliens in the most recent elections of 2016 and 2018, not the Russians. Russians and Chinese, whether state actors, businesses, or simply with foreign individuals wanting to play games apparently were involved in influence peddling or election manipulation on some level, but it pales in relation to that perpetrated by illegal aliens and those parties and party position seekers who encourage them to vote.

That is voter fraud, aiding and abetting voter fraud, and anyone caught doing it must be punished. The Gray Zone demands it in order to restore public confidence to our electoral process.

Congressional Representation

There is a storm brewing over counting illegal aliens including DACA children in the 2020 Census. The Secretary of Commerce, U. S. Department of Commerce, Ross plans to add one additional question to the census: "Is this person a citizen of the United States?" California of course is fighting the placement of that question in the courts all the way to the Supreme Court. For reference the question was on forms once upon a time, but the last time was 1950.

The reason it is critical to California is 28% of household residents there have an illegal alien living with them. The number is much higher in the Los Angeles area and would affect population representation for the House of Representatives in the U.S. Congress. The change also would affect federal funding for everything from schools to transportation.

(Supreme Count weighs census question that could undercut California's Power, <u>Los Angeles Times</u> (via TNS), February 15, 2019 as reported by David G. Savage in the <u>Daily Republic</u>, Fairfield-Suisun, CA.)

News reports (February and March 2019) that I watched on news casts and heard on the radio reported that 75,000 illegal immigrants attempted to enter the U.S. one month and 100,000 the next. That would project to 1.2 million in 2019. This is untenable, debilitating, expensive, and a waste!

Legal Immigration

By default, it seems we have accepted legal immigration from countries previously restricted, but with the doors thrown open to resettlement by the prior administration to groups with values antithetical to Americans and flowing from the Middle East. These groups of mostly Muslims have become an inner threat to the peace, security and welfare of all Americans.

Table 6-3: Fiscal Year 2013 Welfare Rates[21]

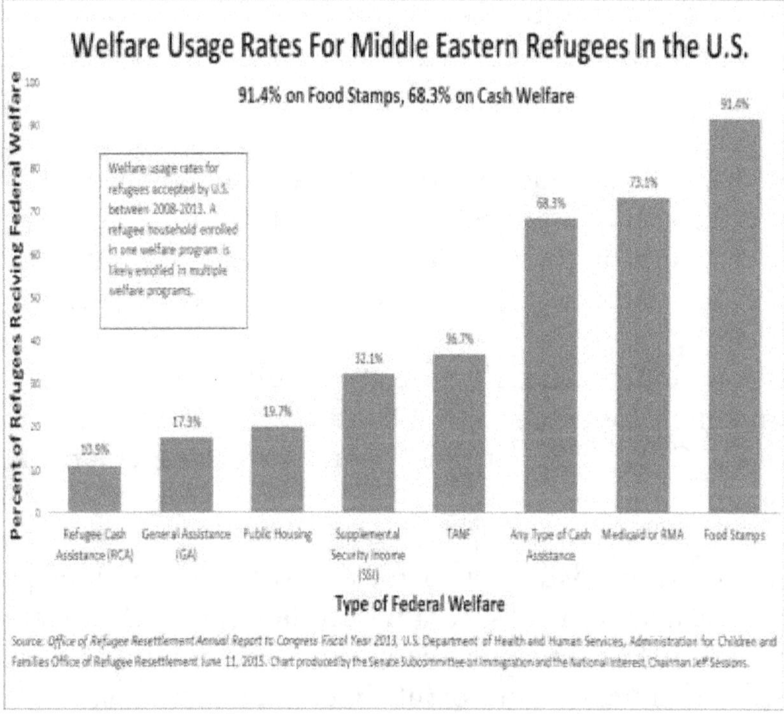

The welfare cost is obviously excessive and disproportionate to the rest of society.

Debatable Propositions

1. The flow of illegal immigrants must be stopped to provide security for those of us in the Gray Zone through stopping

welfare payments directly or independently, preserving American sovereignty, stopping the excessive amount of all crimes, especially violent ones, from being perpetrated on American citizens whether or not in the Gray Zone and preventing diseased vectors from spreading horrific diseases throughout our country to us, our children and grandchildren.

2. Illegal immigrants must not receive any Medicaid or Medicare funding of any kind, nor funding support of any kind. Logic tells us they come only for the money, not to be Americans. Only citizens meaning those born in the U.S. to U.S. citizens and those born abroad of U.S. citizens on government, business, or travel may receive any benefits or entitlements

3. Voter fraud laws must be strengthened and stiff penalties exercised for aiding and abetting their voting and conspiring to skew votes through identification documents of any kind. Only U.S. citizens may vote in any elections.

4. It is fair and reasonable to put the question on census questionnaires of whether or not there are illegal aliens in the household. Only U.S. citizens count for representational purposes in Congress.

5. Begin returning Muslims to the Middle East to stabilize their regions and countries from which they came. They were not properly vetted and must be done on an individual basis as soon as possible by teams of intelligence professionals.

Chapter 7

SECURITY AND SELF DEFENSE

Senior Citizens need guns to give them a psychological advantage and a quick physical reaction one. ~Roy E. Peterson

"The right of the citizens to keep and bear arms has justly been considered as the palladium of the Republic, since it offers a strong moral check against the usurpation and arbitrary power of rulers; and will generally, even if these are successful in the first instance, enable the people to resist and triumph over them. ~Joseph Story, Associate Justice of the U.S. Supreme Court and Founder of Harvard Law School.

Everyone who believes in strict interpretation of the United States Constitution is a moderate. ~Roy E. Peterson

The 2nd Amendment to the U.S. Constitutio

The 2nd Amendment to the Constitution of the United States is the shortest, most direct and the Amendment least subject to interpretation:

> "A well-regulated Militia, being necessary to the
> security of a free State, the right of the people to
> keep and bear Arms, shall not be infringed."[1]

The first half is one rationale. The guts of the amendment are pure and simple. All in one sentence and that is not by accident either. No infringement! Yet for the past decade Congress tries to pass legislation banning one type of firearm, or another. Many of them thought erroneously that the AR in the AR-15 stood for Automatic Rifle. That is wrong.

It stands for the Armalite Company that manufactures

them. The AR-15 rifle is a frequent target partly for this reason, partly because it has been employed in some mass shootings, and partly because it was made for the military, so it must be terrible. It is a semiautomatic weapon, not that it matters. No infringement means no laws against it.

I have a theory on the order of Amendments to the Bill of Rights. That is, they were placed in order of importance to the Founding Fathers and to us (the people). The fact that the right to keep and bear arms is the 2nd Amendment is no accident in the placement of amendments in the order of most importance. The stipulation that it shall not be abridged means that neither Congress nor the President, nor the States have any authority to place any control PERIOD.

AMAC and AARP have a differing approach to upholding the rights of Gray Zoners regarding self-defense and home protection. AARP advocates against the 2nd Amendment for modified gun control including the more aged of the population. AMAC takes the moderate approach of holding true to the tenets of the 2nd Amendment that the right to keep and bear arms shall not be abridged.

The uninitiated will note that sometimes I speak of guns and sometimes rifles as if they were different. They are. One of the first things I learned in the military was to make the proper distinction. In the first training class the Sergeant held up a pistol and said, "This is your gun." Then he held up a long-barreled weapon and said, "This is your rifle. Don't forget the difference." The word "arms" in the 2nd Amendment covers both.

Stop Messing with the 2nd Amendment

I get it! Congress thinks it should do something to halt mass shootings, especially in schools. This is where my slogan of "one is too many" comes back to me. I agree that one is too many; however, it is not to be constrained or solved by gun controls. This is a human mental problem that requires various approaches including arming guards and/or teachers at schools to defend the students. Put the focus where it belongs and make plans to combat the problem. That includes handling of guns and rifles taught in the schools and the need to respect them

Statistics for Those Who Need Them

I know I am going to have to present some statistics soon demonstrating the need and reasonableness of such a logical thought, since there are those who will just "shoot their mouths and criticisms back" as if they were waiting to toss a hand grenade, or attempt to shoot down logic just to be argumentative.

Statistics, especially regarding the use of guns/rifles/arms, is a set of data that can be used to show almost anything depending on what is included in the numbers and the assumptions made. One must separate suicides from murders, for example. For your information the choice of devices in suicides is hand guns. In a sense that may be a more humane way to go if a person has an intent to commit suicide.

Most critics begin with percentage of crime involving guns in the United States versus other countries and show how much higher that is here than in other developed countries. There is a logic disconnect here for those who believe getting rid of guns would get rid of gun violence. That logical disconnect is from reality.

There are various estimates of guns and/or gun owners in the U.S. I will start with hundreds of millions.

Where there are guns freely allowed in this country the statistics drop to similar and lower levels. Here is one map that will show it, that you can find in color on the Internet, but has to be black, gray and white here:

<u>**Table 7-1: FBI Statistics for Gun Violence, 2014[2]**</u>

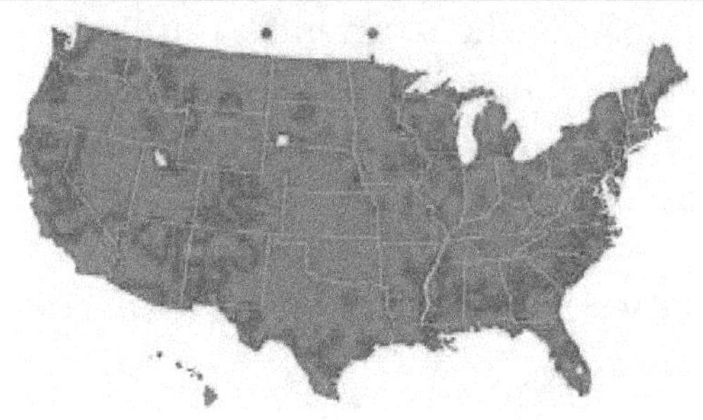

There is an interesting correlation between the map of FBI Statistics above for 2014 and Table 2 below that is the Electoral Map of the Presidential Election in 2016. The correlation is the same parts of the country for the most part that freely allow guns are the same ones that voted for Trump to be President in the 2016 election.

<u>**Table 7-2: Electoral Map Presidential Election 2016[3]**</u>

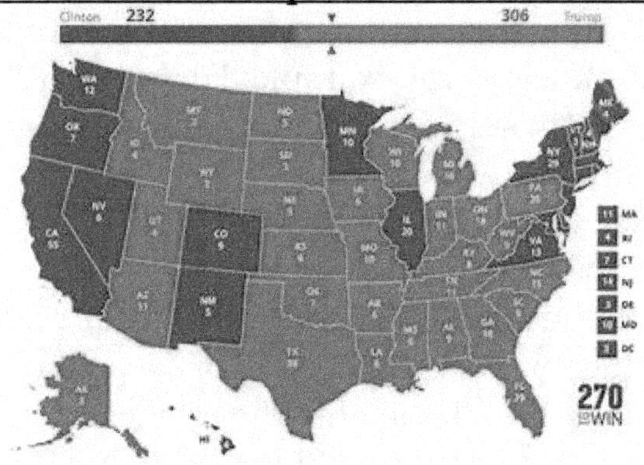

In the third table below, the average number of people in the U.S.A. killed by rifles is 260.8 over the six years from 2012 to 2017. You may ask, what about 2018?

The answer is the FBI does not provide the data until September after the end of the year. That means 2018 data will not be available until September 2019.

2012 CRIME CLOCK STATISTICS

A Violent Crime occurred every	26.0 seconds
One Murder every	35.4 minutes
One Forcible Rape every	6.2 minutes
One Robbery every	1.5 minutes
One Aggravated Assault every	41.5 seconds
A Property Crime occurred every	3.5 seconds
One Burglary every	15.0 seconds
One Larceny-theft every	5.1 seconds
One Motor Vehicle Theft every	43.7 seconds

There is a completely positive correlation between the states and/or areas of states that have guns and low gun violence. This is where statisticians make a case on either side by extension or deletion of numbers to make their case, thus throwing the rest of us into a spiral and hoodwinking Congress.

Here is the deal. Read each table and statistic carefully and think about whether they are comparing similar data, or apples to oranges. In this process one side comes up with a set of statistics to suggest that where guns are tightly controlled there is less gun violence, but they forget that the majority of crime and murder with firearms is in the big cities. New York, Chicago and Detroit are historically at the top of the list. Note the tight regulation of both states and cities in the cases of New York/New York, Chicago/Illinois, Detroit/Michigan, and Baltimore/Maryland. One must separate suicide by guns (high), overall crime with guns (medium), homicides by guns (medium), homicides by rifle (minimal), and accidental deaths from guns (extremely low). Those that attempt to regulate them much tighter or ban them by laws that are against the 2nd Amendment and should be overturned. With logic in our arsenal I can confidently state that controlling guns raises the level of gun violence, while gun friendly regions radically decrease gun violence for the most part!

Table 7-4: Homicides/Firearms/Rifles 2006-2017[5]

Year	# Homicides	Firearm Homicides	Death by Rifles*
2017	17,284	10,982	353
2016	17,250	11,004	371
2015	15,883	9,778	258
2014	14,164	8,312	258
2013	14,319	8,454	285
2012	14,856	8,897	298
2010	14,722	8,874	x
2009	15,399	9,199	x
2008	16,485	9,528	x
2007	17,128	10,129	x
2006	17,309	10,225	x

***Death by Rifle includes "mass" shootings.**
FBI does not report previous year until September

First note the number of deaths from rifles. The average over a six-year period is 261 and about one-third of those were mass shootings. Almost no one uses a rifle to commit a crime or homicide.

Depending on the year one can take the U.S. population and come up with statistics indicating that gun violence does not even make the top 50 reasons for death in the United States, even the top 60. Again, given the year and data, overall gun violence kills on average between .010-.018% of the approximate 2.5 million who die each year in the United

States. See the National Center for Health Studies and Medical News Today and then you may compare them with the FBI Crime Statistics.[6]

The National Center for Health Studies provides the top 10 causes of death in the United States for 2016:[7]

<u>Table 7-5: Causes of Death in the US (Most to Least)</u>[7]

- Heart disease: 635,260
- Cancer: 598,038
- Accidents (unintentional injuries): 161,374
- Chronic lower respiratory diseases: 154,596
- Stroke (cerebrovascular diseases): 142,142
- Alzheimer's disease: 116,103
- Diabetes: 80,058
- Influenza and pneumonia: 51,537
- Nephritis, nephrotic syndrome, and nephrosis: 50,046
- Intentional self-harm (suicide): 44,965

<u>Medical News Today</u> reports that "nearly 75 percent of all deaths in the United States are attributed to just ten causes, with the top three of these accounting for over 50 percent of all deaths.[8]

The Case of Mass Shootings

The number of mass shootings in the United States is extremely low, however, they receive the most political attention. Note the column in the chart above that I copied out of FBI statistics.

The RAND Corporation had the same problem I was thinking about and that is how many does it take to have a mass shooting? Their conclusions on the numbers were depending on the data source and the definitions used by the source, "there were seven, 65, 332, or 371 mass shootings in the United States in 2015." This is because "The U.S. government has never defined *mass shooting*, and there is no single universally accepted definition of the term. The Federal Bureau of Investigation's definition of a mass murderer requires at least four casualties, excluding the offender or offenders, in a single incident. Public law (the Investigative Assistance for Violent Crime Act of 2012; Pub. L. 112-265) defines a *mass killing* as a single incident in which three or more people were killed. Alternative definitions include two or more injured victims or four or more people injured or killed, including the shooter."[9]

10 LOGICAL REASONS TO LEAVE THE 2ND AMENDMENT ALONE

I have placed ten logical reasons for maintaining the 2nd Amendment in alphabetical order. I did that, since they should all be accorded equal weight in the thought process and placing them in alphabetical order gives them that same sense of priority. From a graduate study course, I assure you that these are some of the additional reasons, and not just for the purpose of maintaining the Militia.

1. Assisting Law Enforcement

Fred Foy was the radio voice that introduced episodes of "The Lone Ranger." Several lines into the introduction he said, "Return with us now to those thrilling days of yester year." That fits this first logical category of assisting law enforcement, since the ability to do so was prevalent in all the radio and TV cowboy series from The Lone Ranger to Roy Rogers, Gene Autry, The Cisco Kid, and Hopalong Cassiday. There were the cowboy heroes, sidekicks, and usually a posse all ready to assist law enforcement as needed with their guns and rifles.

This is still an important reason today for keeping guns near and handy, especially when a deranged shooter or terrorist is on the prowl. Armed civilians likely are the closest to the action and the ones who can do the most to prevent a mass shooting, or at least stop it as soon as possible.

Personal Story. A beloved member of our hometown in West Texas was a Texas Highway Patrolman named Sammy Long. Sammy received a call on his radio that a California felon who escaped from prison was somewhere out in West Texas. Sammy found the felon in a car with California license plates and stopped him. The felon shot Sammy and Sammy perished. Nearby was a citizen with a gun who immediately took aim and killed the convict with a hail of bullets. The entire town mourned the death of its friend and protector. The man who shot the escaped convict was given awards by the Texas Department of Public Safety and his name was withheld from the media, but he not only came to the defense of Sammy, he took out the person responsible and helped keep the community safe.

I have a proposal for Gray Zone citizens to be permanently deputized by the Governor as a posse for the Texas Rangers and be available on call.

2. Deterrent to Crime

While I am on the topic of my home area, rifles are carried on gun racks inside the pickup trucks of everyone from young kids to oilfield workers. A shooting death is rare in West Texas. Compare that to Chicago, Detroit, Los Angeles, New York, or any of our cities that attempt to limit them and get them out of the hands of civilians. Guns and rifles are an obvious deterrent to crime. Logic tells me that, just as it should tell you.

3. Food Acquisition

For many poor families the only way to put meat on the table is hunting game. This was especially true in the past, but it still applies to tens of thousands of farm families who need to supplement their animal husbandry that pays the bills with fresh meat acquired at little cost with a few bullets or shotgun shells.

Personal story. I asked my dad one time why he hunted on occasion. The answer was to kill a pig or cow meant less money for the family. The other option was fishing which I also learned to do at an early age. For Thanksgiving we often had pheasant that my dad brought home from a hunt, often from our own farm in South Dakota.

Logic tells me that in tough times the only way to survive comes through the barrel of a rifle. A bullet or shotgun shell is a lot cheaper than going to a grocery store.

4. Law of Unintended Consequences

The law of unintended consequences is that actions that are taken even with careful planning may have the opposite effect in the near or long term that were not anticipated. The term was first introduced to me in college as a theory postulated by the social scientist, Robert K. Merton. Variables that were unforeseen may affect the final outcome and in fact that may be 180 degrees from the intended one.

In the case of gun and rifle control measures, we can foresee the consequences, yet pressure is continual by anti-gun legislators to take away guns from Americans, especially when there is a school or mass shooting. The unintended consequence, which in this case is not only foreseeable, but demonstrated by historical example after historical example is a potential surge in violence against decent citizens by criminals and state authorities leading to eventual dictatorship.

Some of the strongest examples are these dictators are: Stalin, Hitler, Mao and Castro. For the new millennials who do not know history these were all Socialist/Communist dictators.

5. Oppressive Government

The writers and voters on the establishment of the U.S. Constitution were adamant that one of the reasons for the 2nd Amendment was to give the people the right to rebel against illicit and tyrannous government should the new Republic become beset with such a plague. That is also why they included the phrase, "whenever government becomes destructive of these things, it shall be the right of the people to alter or abolish it..."

Here is a sample of quotes numbered in consecutive order on the importance of arms to the Founding Fathers and those of influence in the days of the founding of our new Republic:

Thomas Jefferson, of Virginia:

1. "No free man shall ever be debarred the use of arms." — Proposed Virginia Constitution, 1776.

2. "Laws that forbid the carrying of arms. . . disarm only those who are neither inclined nor determined to commit crimes. . . Such laws make things worse for the assaulted and better for the assailants; they serve rather to encourage than to prevent homicides, for an unarmed man may be attacked with greater confidence than an armed man." — Jefferson's "Commonplace Book," 1774-1776, quoting from On Crimes and Punishment, by criminologist Cesare Beccaria, 1764.

George Mason, of Virginia:

3. "[W]hen the resolution of enslaving America was formed in Great Britain, the British Parliament was advised by

an artful man, who was governor of Pennsylvania, to disarm the people; that it was the best and most effectual way to enslave them; but that they should not do it openly, but weaken them, and let them sink gradually.". . . I ask, who are the militia? They consist now of the whole people, except a few public officers." — Virginia`s U.S. Constitution ratification convention, 1788

Samuel Adams, of Massachusetts:

4. "The said Constitution [shall] be never construed to authorize Congress to infringe the just liberty of the press, or the rights of conscience; or to prevent the people of the United States, who are peaceable citizens, from keeping their own arms." — Massachusetts: U.S. Constitution ratification convention, 1788.

5. "If ye love wealth more than liberty, the tranquility of servitude greater than the animating contest for freedom, go home and leave us in peace. We seek not your council, nor your arms. Crouch down and lick the hand that feeds you; and may your chains set lightly upon you, and posterity forget that ye were our country men." - Samuel Adams, 1776.

Richard Henry Lee, of Virginia:

6. "A militia when properly formed are in fact the people themselves . . . and include all men capable of bearing arms. . . To preserve liberty, it is essential that the whole body of people always possess arms... The mind that aims at a select militia, must be influenced by a truly anti-republican principle." — Additional Letters From The Federal Farmer, 1788.

James Madison, of Virginia:

7. The Constitution preserves "the advantage of being armed which Americans possess over the people of almost every other nation. . . (where) the governments are afraid to trust the people with arms." — <u>The Federalist, No. 46</u>.

8. The right of the people to keep and bear arms shall not be infringed. A well-regulated militia, composed of the body of the people, trained to arms, is the best and most natural defense of a free country," – James Madison, I Annals of Congress 434, June 8, 1789.

Tench Coxe, of Pennsylvania:

9. "The militia, who are in fact the effective part of the people at large, will render many troops quite unnecessary. They will form a powerful check upon the regular troops, and will generally be sufficient to over-awe them." — <u>An American Citizen</u>, Oct. 21, 1787.

10. "Who are the militia? Are they not ourselves? Congress have no power to disarm the militia. Their swords and every other terrible implement of the soldier, are the birthright of an American . . .. The unlimited power of the sword is not in the hands of either the federal or state governments, but, where I trust in God it will ever remain, in the hands of the people." — <u>The Pennsylvania Gazette</u>, Feb. 20, 1788.

11. "As the military forces which must occasionally be raised to defend our country, might pervert their power to the injury of their fellow citizens, the people are confirmed by the next article (of amendment) in their right to keep and bear their private arms." — <u>Federal Gazette</u>, June 18, 1789.

Noah Webster, of Pennsylvania:

12. "Before a standing army can rule, the people must be disarmed; as they are in almost every kingdom in Europe. The supreme power in America cannot enforce unjust laws by the sword; because the whole body of the people are armed, and constitute a force superior to any band of regular troops that can be, on any pretense, raised in the United States. A military force, at the command of Congress, can execute no laws, but such as the people perceive to be just and constitutional; for they will possess the power." — <u>An Examination of The Leading Principles of the Federal Constitution</u>, Philadelphia, 1787.

Alexander Hamilton, of New York:

13. "[I]f circumstances should at any time oblige the government to form an army of any magnitude, that army can never be formidable to the liberties of the people while there is a large body of citizens, little if at all inferior to them in discipline and the use of arms, who stand ready to defend their rights and those of their fellow citizens." — The Federalist, No. 29.

14. "Little more can reasonably be aimed at with respect to the people at large than to have them properly armed and equipped." - Alexander Hamilton (Federalist Papers #29).

Thomas Paine, of Pennsylvania:

15. "[A]rms discourage and keep the invader and plunderer in awe, and preserve order in the world as well as property. . . Horrid mischief would ensue were the law-abiding deprived of the use of them." — <u>Thoughts On Defensive War</u>, 1775.

Fisher Ames, of Massachusetts:

16. "The rights of conscience, of bearing arms, of changing the government, are declared to be inherent in the people." — <u>Letter to F.R. Minoe</u>, June 12, 1789.

Elbridge Gerry, of Massachusetts:

17. "What, sir, is the use of militia? It is to prevent the establishment of a standing army, the bane of liberty. . . Whenever Government means to invade the rights and liberties of the people, they always attempt to destroy the militia, in order to raise a standing army upon its ruins." — <u>Debate, U.S. House of Representatives</u>, August 17, 1789.

Patrick Henry, of Virginia:

18. "Guard with jealous attention the public liberty. Suspect everyone who approaches that jewel." — <u>Virginia`s U.S. Constitution ratification convention</u>.

George Washington to Congress:

19. "A free people ought not only to be armed, but disciplined…" – George Washington, First Annual Address to both Houses of Congress, January 8, 1790.

Reverend Nicholas Collin:

20. "While the people have property, arms in their hands, and only a spark of noble spirit, the most corrupt Congress must be mad to form any project of tyranny." - Rev. Nicholas Collin, <u>Fayetteville Gazette </u>(N.C.), October 12, 1789.

Pennsylvania Gazette:

21. "... the loyalists in the beginning of the late war, who objected to associating, arming and fighting, in defense of our liberties, because these measures were not constitutional. A free people should always be left... with every possible power to promote their own happiness." - <u>Pennsylvania Gazette</u>, April 23, 1788.

John Adams:

22. "Arms in the hands of citizens (may) be used at individual discretion...in private self-defense..." -John Adams, 1788 <u>A DEFENSE OF THE CONSTITUTION OF THE GOVERNMENT OF THE USA</u>, p.471.

These are 22 quotes from those who were either Founding Fathers and wrote their thoughts in **The Federalist Papers**, or were significant influencers on public opinion of the day.

I will give you a more recent quote by a respected Democratic President, John F. Kennedy who said,-"By calling attention to 'a well-regulated militia,' 'the security of the nation,' and the right of each citizen 'to keep and bear arms,' our founding fathers recognized the essentially civilian nature of our economy...The Second Amendment still remains an important declaration of our civilian-military relationships in which every citizen must be ready to participate in the defense of his country. For that reason, I believe the Second Amendment will always be important."[10]

Now I add back in the quote that began the Chapter. Joseph Story, an early Associate Justice of the U.S. Supreme Court and Founder of Harvard Law School stated, "The right of the citizens to keep and bear arms has justly been considered as the palladium of the Republic, since it offers a strong moral check against the usurpation and arbitrary power of rulers; and will generally, even if these are successful in the first instance, enable the people to resist and triumph over them."[11]

6. Prevention of Invasion

The prevention of invasion is something that may have saved the American mainland from attack by Japan at the start of World War II. There is one unsubstantiated quote that may have come from the papers of Gordon W. Prange, Historian, Staff of Douglas MacArthur that quoted "Japan's Admiral Isoroku Yamamoto as saying: "You cannot invade mainland United States. There would be a rifle behind each blade of grass."[12]

Regardless of whether the quote was a verbal one or lost in some papers after World War II, I believe that armed Americans were a deterrent and that Japan had sufficient human intelligence assets on the West Coast to warn against such an attack, since the coast was bristling with arms and ammunition. It is the reason Texans are so confident of preventing the government from taking away any gun rights and stand ready to repel the illegal immigrants with just a word from someone in authority.

The same thing applies to any thoughts of being attacked by Cuba, Russia, China, or any other foe over the decades. This is still one of our greatest assets and deterrent to invasion by another country. If we did not have weapons, we would have been invaded long ago by Mexico looking to avenge their losses.

7. Property Protection

In a free society every individual has the right to protect the things he cherishes from attack, whether it be a business, a church, a home, a farm, or any other personal property. Yes, I included church attacks as something we have the right to protect against.

It should be a given that I need write no further utterance on this topic, except I am angry that some crooks have sued for trespassing and committing grand larceny on another person's property and then being shot in the dark by the owner. That cannot happen in a free society!

8. Reserve Trained Manpower for War

The most difficult problem of World War I and World War II in the first instance was finding anyone from the city who knew how to shoot a firearm and do so safely. Fortunately, there were country folk like Audie Murphy and Sergeant York that could take on the enemy and the training of troops in marksmanship. There is no substitute for feeling the rifle recoil and concentrating on the target to squeeze off a round and have it hit the target. In the past there was a draft for entrance onto active duty with the military in the American Revolution, American Civil War, World War I and II, and the Cold War that took us through Korea and Vietnam. Conscription, as the main term used, was phased out in 1973, at the end of the Vietnam War due to protests, draft evasions, and the potential for a more loyal fighting force that was better paid, trained, and committed to the mission of defending the country.

Conscription was a great bonding factor for all classes of men, since it was not a respecter of status or station in life, although I am aware of those who found ways to beat the system such as Bill Clinton remaining in England. The all-volunteer force has done well in providing a standing army, but has lost the leavening effect of reaching the middle and upper classes, except for those with a sense of patriotic duty.

I am one who believes it is even more imperative to be prepared now and at least one summer should be spent by high school and college men and women if so desired to engage in marksmanship practice and basic military drill and discipline. Six weeks would accomplish that task and provide a base for a better rounded, disciplined person for society.

The Selective Service system has remained in place and all male citizens are required to register between the ages of 18 and 25. The reason for remaining in place is a national emergency that may require a rapid call to duty.

9. Self Defense

As with several of these points, the reason should be obvious to the casual observer that the topic provides an inviolate proposition that is a primary defense of an action with a gun in a legal case before a judge and jury.

The far left will claim that with authorities having a monopoly on guns, violent crime will be prevented. That would be true only if there was a complete reformation of society and men were good, drugs were removed as a motivating force for theft, money was eliminated as a root cause for evil, and everyone was taught the proper morals in school and the home. As with all things on the left, society does not operate that way, or if it did, it was only for a short while in history where there was a cohesive group and word traveled rapidly of anyone's misdeeds that would shame themselves and their family members.

The right will claim that preventive action is justified to take out a possible threat. This is a reactionary method and one thankfully not sanctioned.

Moderates like myself have the perspective of not only imminent danger, but a gun pointed at us with a perceived threat to kill us justifies the use of any arm available whether they are approaching with a pick axe, poison dart, or knife, let alone a gun or rifle.

10. Varmints

The temptation is to include two-legged varmints, but I limit this category to things that crawl and slither like snakes, things that fly like chicken hawks, and things that eat eggs and chickens like skunks and foxes. Living on a farm as I did, the threat of economic loss is considerable from varmints. When I was eight years old or so, I knew one of our hens liked to nest and produce eggs under our corn picker parked in the center of the granary. I was young and skinny, so my mother let me crawl under the corn picker and get the eggs.

Egg collection was one of my chores. One day, as I crawled underneath, I met a skunk face-to-face. I grabbed the eggs the skunk was about to eat and fled the picker and shed without getting sprayed. I ran to my mom shouting that I met a skunk. If dad were home, he would have tracked it down and finished it off with the .22 rifle. If my mom would have allowed me to learn to shoot by then, I would have done it myself. My mother did not let me shoot anything, including a BB gun or bow and arrow until I was ten. I asked for a BB gun every Christmas, but never got one.

Does anyone really think we should have to do without firearms to eliminate the varmint form of thievery? Logic tells us that firearms beat arrows, BB guns and stones.

I have just taken you through ten logical reasons why the 2nd Amendment must never be neutered. They are all logical and rational. They are the moderate center positions.

Chapter 8

FOOD SAFETY

"We don't really have any(one) that protect(s) the food supply from farm to table. We have a food safety system that's piecemeal, largely divided between two agencies (USDA and FDA) that don't talk to each other very much. Neither agency can enforce regulations from the farm to the table." ~Marion Nestle

We trusted government with our food safety. They broke it again.
~Roy E. Peterson.

Food for those of us in the Gray Zone, presents new challenges to survival. Listeria, Salmonella, bacteria and other food infections and infestations, while not limited to our age group, certainly become increasingly dangerous. To that mix we have developed diseases that are caused by salt intake, sugar consumption and alcohol use and abuse. What we eat and drink may increase our personal health issues, disable us, and kill us prematurely. Our internal organs are compromised, our stomachs turn against us and our food habits haunt us.

Prescription drugs like those opioid-based warn the effects may cause constipation and have side effects that can increase potential for death, though life may not be worth living without them taking care of our aches, pains, and fragilities. Don't you just love those commercials that provide the side effects, as if they were easy to toss out of our minds? Then they begin with something like, "If you are allergic to this medicine don't take it." Next, they will tell you that in some cases this medicine can lead to early death. "Talk to your doctor about it!" That is equaled only by the advertisement of attorneys that intimate if you die or died, we will represent you. We do know what they mean, but it is funny to see and hear them on our television sets.

Americans should be disturbed that our government laws and oversight are compromised, that our food supply chain is being penetrated with foreign food products, that labeling of meat sources has recently regressed to meet World Trade Organization decisions in which originations are improperly labeled. Of all the things those of us in the Gray Zone thought about our food, the last thing we suspected was hiding things from us, or at least making them deceptive, because of a ruling outside our jurisdiction that impinges on American sovereignty.

We want to know whether or not our beef comes solely from American cattle raised on American soil, processed by American food product companies owned by American businesses and not cut with any foreign grown product. We have that right to know so that we can make our own choices to reward our local American workers and sources, not those coming from anywhere else.

Personal story. I went into an HEB grocery store in Texas the other day and thought I purchased a product of the USA, since it had a label on it that said USDA prime. I was going to eat the ribs after barbecuing them, but in the fine print I saw a marking "CR" in another place on the label in black ink. I realized the meat must have come from Costa Rica and threw it out.

We want government to intercept any food borne illnesses like the listeria infections that were caught early from lettuce crops recently, but we want it to be prior to consumption. When I say "caught early" it was after retail sales and the sickening of a lot of people in widespread areas in the meantime.

Listeria in the Blue Bell ice cream in 2015, shut them down. Since Texans have a fondness for Blue Bell ice cream, we all had to wait patiently for them to reopen to get one of our favorite treats.

Foreign produce and food products have become a staple in our supply chain, but I, for one, want to know if my tomatoes came from Mexico, my catfish came from Vietnam and my grapes came from Chile. I am particularly sensitive to beef and pork grown elsewhere. Fortunately, when I go to the grocery store, some of the produce like tomatoes have a little sticker on each one telling me where it was grown. We do have the government to thank for enforcement of some of the issues we may have.

Then there is the basic issue of the safety of our water. We all know that contaminates were in the water in Flint, Michigan, among other cities and towns. We also learned that the ground water around military facilities had radioactive contaminates leaching into them causing abnormal spikes in cancer in military families that live in post or base housing.

USDA Inspection Responsibilities

The U.S. Department of Agriculture handles food safety and labeling of literally everything "from soup to nuts," including meat sources and processing. According to some accounts the USDA receives 80% of the funding for safety and handling, while the Food and Drug Administration (FDA) receives 20% of the funds, yet the FDA overall is responsible for 80% of the products consumers use.[1]

Worse than that, one of the key authors writing on food safety and inspections said, "To speak only of food inspections: The United States currently imports 80% of its seafood, 32% of its fruits and nuts, 13% of its vegetables, and 10% of its meats. In 2007, these foods arrived in 25,000 shipments a day from about 100 countries. The FDA was able to inspect about 1% of these shipments, down from 8% in 1992. In contrast, the USDA is able to inspect 16% of the foods under its purview. By one assessment, the FDA has become so short-staffed that it would take the agency 1,900 years to inspect every foreign plant that exports food to the United States."[1]

Should I be worried about my food supply as a member of the Gray Zone? Absolutely, and also worried about the food supply for pets. I suggest reading Marion Nestle's book, <u>Pet Food Politics: The Chihuahua in the Coal Mine</u>, that I cited in endnote #1, above, for a horror story on a pet food recall in Canada of a brand with a lot of purchasers in the United States and her loss of a pet due to not getting the word.[1] Marion Nestle is an American academic. She is the Paulette Goddard Professor of Nutrition, Food Studies, and Public Health at New York University. She is also a professor of Sociology at NYU and a visiting professor of Nutritional Sciences at Cornell University.

<u>Beef and Pork</u>

I remembered from my university graduate courses a book entitled, The Jungle, by Upton Sinclair. The item I remembered most was that grocers who had a lot of sawdust for cleaning butcher counter floors in those day would add sawdust to the hamburger for cheap weight additives. I never forgot that image. Retracing my thoughts while conducting research online, I was able to reconstruct what I remembered. The book was published as a serial in 1904 in one of the Socialist newspapers of the time, <u>Appeal to Reason</u>, and in novel form in 1906 by Doubleday.

According to the <u>Encyclopedia Britannica</u>, Upton Sinclair was a Socialist who was intent on exposing dangerous working conditions of workers and simultaneously the inhumane treatment of animals. Sinclair went "undercover for seven weeks inside various Chicago meatpacking plants." As one of the "muckrakers" his story in novel form reflected the true conditions of the plants and the sordid processing of American consumer beef. Contrary to his intentions, readers came away with concern for the safety of their food.

In his own words as quoted in the <u>Encyclopedia Britannica</u> he said, "I aimed at the public's heart, and by accident I hit it in the stomach."[2] Theodore Roosevelt, then President of the United States used his novel and other muckraking efforts to push through Congress the first Pure Food and Drug Act and the Meat Inspection Act. The Pure Food and Drug Act ensure sanitary processing methods were used in meatpacking plants. The Meat Inspection Act required the U.S. Department of Agriculture to inspect all livestock prior to slaughter.[2]

What Happened to our COOL Laws?

The U.S. Department of Agriculture (USDA) Food Inspection Service (FSIS) is responsible for the labeling, or lack thereof, of meat and meat products. The FSIS operates in accordance with laws passed by Congress. Between 2009 and 2016, Americans finally had a Country-of-Origin (COOL) labeling law on the books after decades of lobbying by ranchers, meat producers, and consumer groups. Then the roof caved in again in 2016. What happened to our COOL Laws?

The World Trade Organization (WTO) is what happened to our COOL Laws, just as the WTO caused other problematic responses by Congress negotiating the world of international trade since we sponsored and joined the WTO on January 1, 1995. While there have been beneficial rulings for the United States, meat labeling is not one of them. While some consumers were upset, the aforementioned interest groups were incensed enough to bring suit against the USDA in 2016.

Beginning in March of 2016, the USDA revoked regulations requiring imported meat products to have COOL labels clearly showing that any slaughtered meat from other countries be so marked, leaving once again the importation of meat to be sold on the same playing field with U.S. meat products blind-siding consumers.

The Ranchers-Cattlemen Action Legal Fund, United Stockgrowers of America, the nation's largest group of independent cattle producers, and the Cattle Producers of Washington did the suing "seeking to force meat to again be labeled if it's produced in other countries and imported to the United States."[3] Their grievance was that the lower cost imported meat products reduced market prices, since the new regulations again allowed importation of beef and pork that could be ground into sausage or hamburger meat, for example and still carry the "Product of the USA" label. That was now once again feasible, because the final processing was done in the USA. For the record, 800 million pounds of beef is imported into the U.S. every year.[3]

The background to this legislative and administrative drama was that starting with the farm bill of 2002 known as Public Law 107-171, passed in the George Bush Administration, which was amended by the 2008 farm bill (Public Law 110-146) and came into force March of 2009, "most retail food stores have been required to inform consumers about the country of origin of fresh fruits and vegetables, fish, shellfish, peanuts, pecans, macadamia nuts, ginseng, and ground and muscle cuts of beef, pork, lamb, chicken, and goat."[4] There were other U.S. laws requiring labeling of country-of-origin for imported food products prepackaged for consumers.[4]

The problem was the United States is a member of the WTO. In the past our laws have changed to accommodate determinations and decisions about all our foreign trade as it impacts other nations. They can get together and present a case in the halls of the WTO alleging unfair trade practices. In the case of trade in agricultural produce and meat, "Canada and Mexico challenged U.S. COOL in the World Trade Organization (WTO), arguing that COOL has a trade-distorting impact by reducing the value and number of cattle and hogs shipped to the U.S. market, thus violating WTO trade commitments. In November 2011, the WTO dispute settlement (DS) panel found that COOL treats imported livestock less favorably than U.S. livestock, and does not meet its objective to provide complete information to consumers on the origin of meat products."[4]

The United State appealed and in March 2013, the WTO Board at least reversed the second part of the statement concerning the ability to provide at least some labeling. With continuing hearings in 2014 and 2015, the final outcome was Canada and Mexico requested authorization to retaliate against U.S. imported products in the amount of US $3 billion.[4] This was further revised to US $781 million for Canada and US $2208 million for Mexico.[4] At this point the idea of voluntarily labeling beef, pork and chicken from livestock exclusively born, raised and slaughtered with a U.S. label came into being.[4]

Foreign Company Purchases of American Food Production Companies

The first time I became concerned about American food production companies being purchased by foreign investors, I had a visceral reaction that our food supply just became hostage to a foreign power and that further erosion of our control of food production of all kinds could lead to a food Apocalypse. Apparently, we are not quite there. I did stop buying Smithfield immediately in 2013, when I learned of the acquisition by a Chinese company. I did not want to eat food produced under dirty conditions to be sold in the United States. Since that time, I have discovered that China had a great need for more hogs and hog products and that was the reason for the purchase. That and gaining immediate access to better equipment and methods of production that could be transferable to China.

I still am skeptical, but understand that from other articles written China is not sending ham and bacon to China for cheaper processing and then sending it back to the United States. Here are the facts on the transaction as reported by Politico:[5]

1. Suanghui International Holdings bought Smithfield Foods in 2013.
2. Smithfield is the largest U.S. pork producer.
3. Suanghui International was China's biggest pork producer.
4. The merger was a deal valued at $7.1 billion including debt.
5. Merger approval was from the U.S. Committee on Foreign Investment.
6. Chinese consumer confidence in domestic products had been "rocked."
7. U.S. pork producers are expected to benefit.
8. China is a net importer of pork though they 60% of the world's pigs.
9. Debbie Stabenow, Senate Agriculture Committee Chair expressed concerns that this and future foreign acquisitions collectively could pose a threat to U.S. food security. Stabenow also stated, "Because CFIUS's review includes issues of national security, it is done in secret with no public oversight or transparency,"[5]

Looking beyond just the food issue in this chapter, there have been many efforts to purchase other strategic assets by China including Unocal as a major oil production company and some electronics firms that were actually blocked, largely because word got out and made a lot of Americans angry, as carried out in the press.

I still have not eaten any Smithfield company products that includes their brands they incorporated: Eckrich, Gwaltney and Armour, since the Chinese takeover, although they were my favorite hickory smoked ham. I have found replacements. Since I have discovered about three months ago at the end of 2018 that they were not importing any meat product from China, I may return to eating their products if only to keep some of it out of the hands of the Chinese. I might add, I had the same problem with Tyson's chicken.

<u>Chicken: Organic, Free-Range, or Cooped Up</u>

Chicken is often identified and labeled as organic and/or free range. Cooped Up is my designation for those that do not fit the other two categories. Organic growing and raising standards are government programs that concentrate on the absence of synthetic chemicals and food sources for animals, stipulated outdoors time including "pasture", sunlight, fresh air and freedom of movement, along with lack of use of fertilizers, hormones and antibiotics. "Foods that are "100 percent organic" must meet government standards absolutely, while products with at least 70 percent organic content may assert on their label that they are "made with organic ingredients."[6] Those standards are not just for chickens, but other animals as well. For me, it just seemed that only fruit, vegetables, and chicken had such a designation, although I was aware of a growing interest in such food products.

As a person in the Gray Zone, I assume I am not alone

in thumbing my nose at organic designations, not only because I think everything is organic if it is an organism, but the cost is an added burden that I do not need.

I have the same reaction to the term "free-range." Free-range simply means animals have access to the outdoors and to natural foods like grass and seeds grown there. The USDA only requires producers of "free-range chicken" prove the poultry has been allowed access to the outside during their course of being raised, while other animals must meet the more stringent standards of the sunlight and free pasture movement. The size of the outdoor space is not specified, currently leaving the description somewhat nondescript and subject to interpretation by the producer without much fear of reprisal or fines. Just make sure, I emphasize that free-range does not qualify as organic, although it may help.[6]

Fish

Fish with omega-3 and omega-6 fatty oils are a healthy alternative to red meat. Salmon is a great fish for these and for taste along with a broad range of fish. The most popular fish in the United States these days is Tilapia that lacks the nutrition of a lot of other fish, but is consumed so much because it lacks the fishy smell of other fish. Tilapia is one of the most eaten fish in the United States. The figure in 2010 was 475 million tons.[7] They are grown like a lot of fish these days in cages or ponds. I remember a scare about Tilapia and where it was grown.

Apparently, there is still a problem with country of origin. The United States and surprisingly Mexico and other Latin American countries are fine due to growing conditions and nutrients they are fed and there is no mercury contamination. "Compared with other fish, farmed tilapia contains relatively small amounts of beneficial omega-3 fatty acids, the fish oils that are the main reasons doctors recommend eating fish frequently; salmon has more than 10 times the amount of tilapia. Also, farmed tilapia contains a less healthful mix of fatty acids because the fish are fed corn and soy instead of lake plants and algae, the diet of wild tilapia."[7]

The key is not to eat Tilapia, catfish, or other farmed fish from Southeast Asia, China or Taiwan.[7] "For the moment, Seafood Watch lists tilapia raised in the United States as a 'best choice,' tilapia from Latin America as a "'alternative' and tilapia from China as 'to be avoided.'"[7]

I ate sushi a long time ago, but when I learned waterborne parasites can be in them, not to mention bacteria and chemicals, I stopped. I did not like it anyway. Fish is made to be served hot from a pot or pan in my estimation.

My concern these days, other than mercury and other chemicals lurking in the flesh, are much like for beef and pork. From whence did the fish originate?

Food and Drug Administration

Food Labeling

Food labeling should be a comfort to us in the Gray Zone, but the information is subject to interpretation and to the mathematicians and their algorithms to come up with averages and means. Serving size is based on what these mathematicians believe is the amount people eat and drink at one time. I think they must use the skinniest people they can find to calculate serving size.

Mathematicians then calculate the size of the package and divide by their idealized number to arrive at the number of servings in the container. For some reason that escapes my logic the companies doing the labeling may give you either calories and nutrients for both the whole package and then each serving size, or they may choose to give just the calories and nutrients for one serving. Thus, you will need to calculate your intake by multiplying the servings as you eat or drink. Some of the bottles of juice or cola may in fact have two servings listed, but you may habitually eat or drink it all.

The next thing is the percent of daily value designed to help a person understand the nutrients in each serving. The FDA uses a daily recommended amount that helps the consumer identify if they are getting enough of the right or matching nutrients in their meals.

I have yet to find someone that analyzes this individually on a daily basis. I certainly never have. The FDA blithely does it for those who have both the time and the psychotic mind to do the calculations and keep some kind of running account in their mind, wrist computer, or notepad. The mandated listed items, if they are present or not are as follows:

1. Calories
2. Fats (total, saturated, transfat)
3. Cholesterol
4. Sodium
5. Carbohydrates Ifiber, total sugar, added sugar)
6. Protein
7. Vitamins
8. Minerals

Food and Drug Administration

Alternative Food Labeling

State governments impinged on the ability of a food product company to use accurate words on labels describing their products. For example, Missouri enacted a law making it "illegal to misrepresent a product as meat if it is not 'derived from harvested production livestock or poultry."[9] States have followed suit causing companies to ensure certain designated food packages are sent to certain states. Even though the American consumer is used to the statement of turkey bacon or veggie burger, these would be prohibited in some states on the label.

Milk is another term that has been used for more than animal produced forms. There is almond milk and soy milk. Although they do not lactate "milk" produced by vegetation has long been accepted including milk from the poppy seeds and from the "milkweed."

Targeted cell-meat products that are just coming to market pose a problem for future labeling and marketing. This may concern a lot of members of the Gray Zone as something they do not want to eat. I have already seen it on social media with respondents going crazy over the very idea of any food produced that way. I suggest though that it will be prevalent in our children's and grandchildren's future.

In a <u>USA Today</u> article, the authors argue that the government is ill-prepared to be a linguist and that the FDA should leave well enough alone and let companies market their products with qualifiers like "veggie-burger" and "almond milk."[9]

In any event Gray Zone citizens need to be aware of the differences and assist in making rational decisions about labeling practices, since we may wind up eating and drinking the results.

Drinking Water

The previous administration unleashed a fire storm about water usage when they tried to limit the collection of rainwater. The Gray Zone found that not only absurd, but unimaginable. Farmers collected rain water in barrels for drinking water and shampooing hair, among other things. No one is going to tax or control that!

Chapter 9

CHANGING THE POLITICAL DIALOGUE

We need to elect some people to Congress who are not wealthy and have a real stake in the Social Security System. ~Roy E. Peterson

Since I find it difficult to believe that someone dependent on Social Security will ever again be elected to Congress from the Gray Zone, we are left to pressure Congress, to ask them their positions when running for office regarding Social Security, illegal immigration, their stance on crime, and then to vote accordingly.

Recently one of my friends on social media asked what they could do to change political views and dynamics for the issues they felt important as senior citizens. I certainly understand the feelings of frustration, the seeming lack of response to senior issues and anger at the policies that seem to emanate from local, state and federal governments. These interests are all covered in this book. I had not yet begun to write, so to speak, so I came up with a list. I did not organize it alphabetically and systematize the descriptions. This chapter does just that without going down into the weeds or getting too deep in the sea. Guess what? Many of the ways to send the messages of the Gray Zone is to become actively involved in politics and help make the change.

I have a list of 25 things a senior citizen can do to become active politically. In many of these there is a subset of ways to become involved that are mentioned: These include: 1.) attending, 2.) donating, 3.) joining, 4.) information sharing and 5.) mobilizing.

Where there is a will there is a way. This aphorism particularly applies to becoming active and involved from a political perspective. In alphabetical order here is the list of twenty-five activities any senior citizen can do to apply pressure and to have their voice heard:

1. Advocacy Groups
2. Assistance Groups
3. Attend Town Hall Meetings
4. Attend Political Rallies
5. Blog or Article Writer
6. Book Writer
7. City Council Attendee
8. City Council or County Council Member
9. Club Member
10. Correspondent to Congress and State Legislators
11. County Hearing Attendance
12. County Leadership Position
13. Host/Hostess Meet the Candidate Parties
14. Petition Starter, Marketer or Signer
15. Parade Participant or Watcher
16. Political Campaign Volunteer
17. Precinct Committee Person
18. Precinct Committee Chair
19. Run for Political Office
20. Sign Placer
21. Social Media Master or Maven
22. State Political Committee Member
23. Volunteer Election Official
24. Voter Registration and Voting
25. Wake Up the Family

Most of these opportunities to become involved do not require that much effort. For those who may find it difficult to get outside the home for various reasons such as caring for an ill spouse or for themselves, there are still a number of things that can be done.

I just know some bright person out there is going to ask with how many activities on the list have I been involved. My answer is 23 of the 25. I never have written a blog yet, though I plan to start and I never ran for City or County Office. At the risk of some of you saying aha, now we know your political views, I respond, not so fast, much like Lee Corso on ESPN Gameday for football.

Personal Story. When I was a Graduate Assistant (GA) working on my Ph.D. at the University of Arizona in the late 1960's, I had a lady in my class who was returning in middle age to acquire a teaching degree. Government 100 was required for all teaching certificates at the time in Arizona. Being a GA meant I attended lectures by the Professor two times a week and the third day of the week (usually Friday), I would go over the material in detail to try to fill in gaps the students might have missed, to stimulate independent discussion, and to add substantive material to the lectures.

The pleasant lady, who I remember to this day with the first name of Jackie, in this particular class, came up to me after several weeks and asked what I planned to do with my degree. I said I would like to become a professor and perhaps run for political office someday. She told me they needed a Precinct Committee Person in my precinct and asked if I would run for the position. Of course, I at first demurred and responded that working on my degree did not give me much free time. She said she would get up my petition and all I would have to do is sign it and she would turn it in to the committee that handled those things for the political party.

I ran unopposed and became a Precinct Committee Person. I asked her what I needed to do next and she said the Precinct Chair Person is leaving when they graduate, so you will be the Precinct Chair shortly. You need to attend Political Party meetings in Tucson with me if you can and don't have classes those evenings. I shortly became the Chair and attended the first meeting. I met people interested in running for office at the state and city levels. They gave short speeches to the party faithful mostly about their backgrounds and why they were running. They focused briefly on the issues of the upcoming campaign.

After my third meeting in the third month, Jackie sat next to me and said she proposed my name for the State of Arizona Republican Committee. The list would contain about 120 names that had been proposed, but she said she had talked to a lot of people and was certain I would be selected as one of the 90 members (at that time). I went to the meeting and paid attention as they went through the list. Some were dropped for nonattendance at meetings and others either declined or were crossed off for various reasons. I was selected as the 85th member out of the 90 total and now I was on the State Republican Committee. After the meeting I was talking with Jackie and thanking her. Then I mischievously asked, "When do I run for Governor?" She laughed as did her friends. She knew I had military officer duty that had been deferred and that a year from then I would be away from Arizona possibly for a career. That is exactly what happened.

Remember I said, not so fast. I worked hard as a Precinct Committee Person, especially in advance of elections. In this case there was the 1968 primary for President and the voting came down to Richard Nixon and Nelson Rockefeller. I went to every door of my constituency with a brochure for either of them, campaign pins that I still have and bumper stickers. I was in favor of Nelson Rockefeller over Richard Nixon, but I gave an independent pitch on each if asked and handed out the various items if they had any interest in one candidate or the other. I remained neutral and did not recommend one or the other. The convention had more candidates including Ronald Reagan and Mitt Romney. Several states had their favorite sons that made them more brokers at the convention than serious contenders.

Later came the showdown for the Presidency between Richard Nixon and Hubert Humphrey. Once again, I made a stop at every house soliciting votes, this time with my own reasons why the Republican candidate was the one for whom they should vote. The Governor of Arizona, Jack Williams beat Goddard for a second term. My wife and I were invited to the Governor's Ball in Phoenix, since I was a member of the State Committee.

1. Advocacy Groups

When I worked on my doctorate in Political Science, I took a course on "interest groups." That was the favored term of the times. That has apparently now been superseded by the term "advocacy group." There are other names for the same thing: lobbying group, special interest group, and campaign group. Regardless of the title you get to pay a fee for joining in return for benefits like a credit card with their name on it, insurance policy discounts both up front and then paying on the backend, paraphernalia like mugs and T-shirts, and a lot of other things they believe will get their name out their and increase their lobbying power.

Some of these groups that are "of interest" to senior citizens are ones that focus entirely on issues having to do with the future welfare of the age group such as AARP and AMAC. Other advocacy groups cover particular subjects of interest such as the AAA, American Legion and NRA that have a broader base, but still have political lobbying interests in line, or not inline depending on your political point of view.

Eight Age Focused Advocacy Groups

Amie Clark writes The Senior List from which I obtained most of the information on the eight senior focused groups with political intentions.[1]

60Plus

The 60Plus Association has not disclosed its membership number. They focus unsurprisingly on the 60+ age group. It is free to join and then they seek contributions for their political lobbying efforts. 60Plus was founded for specific interests in their charter, which is less taxes oriented especially on no inheritance taxes, less government involvement in the lives of seniors, and gun rights. 60Plus has a strong conservative alignment.

AARP

The AARP states they have 38 million members as of 2018. Remember I mentioned they dropped the words that AARP stood for in order to reorient their sales and membership pitch on the 50+ age group, dropping the pitch that is for those aged 65 and upwards. Membership costs $12 per year and the spouse is free. They reduced their age for membership from 65 to 50 to broaden their efforts and membership. They have a wide range of benefits and lobby on senior issues of interest. Political orientation is liberal.

ASA

The American Seniors Association was founded in 2005 and has not disclosed its membership. They have a wide range of benefits much like AARP. It is built on five foundations: rebuilding national values, reforming social security, reforming Medicare, reforming the tax code and controlling government spending. They are a conservative organization.

AMAC

The Association of Mature American Citizens was founded in 2007 and has about 1.2 million members.

Membership costs $16 per year and the spouse is free. They primarily in political lobbying. Like AARP they have a wide range of benefits for senior citizens. AMAC was founded specifically for Conservative politically oriented senior citizens.

CAP

The Christian Association of PrimeTimers was founded as a Christian alternative to AARP. Membership age begins at 50 and costs $14.95 a year. Spouses are free. Membership numbers are unreported. Decisions are based on the Christian faith. Members do not have to believe them, just support them, since organizational decisions are made on Christian principles. They have a wide range of benefits for travel and hotels, but specialize in discounts for Christian stores, books and magazines. It is strong Christian Conservative based.

CSA

Christian Seniors Association was founded to lobby on social security issues from a Christian perspective. Membership is $12.95 a year with spouses free. There are no membership numbers released. Founded in 2003 CSA does have insurance plans and a reasonably limited range of benefits including prescription discounts. Political orientation is strong Christian Conservative based.

NAOCS

The National Association of Conservative Seniors promotes military service, small business support, strong family bonds and faith-based living. Memberships are recommended for those 60 and older, but do accept others. First year is free and then $12 per year thereafter. No membership numbers. It was founded in 2012. Political orientation is strong Christian Conservative.

TSC

The Seniors Coalition was first and foremost a public advocacy group focused on repealing the Medicare Catastrophic Coverage Act. Cost in $10 per year/$13 for a couple. No membership numbers. They also have insurance, hotel and prescription discounts. It was founded in 1990 and has over 4 million members. Strong Conservative lean.

Clearly AARP has a size advantage over the rest, so its more liberal orientation is better heard through better funding and onward to campaign contributions. Lobbying power is defined as the message first followed by campaign contributions for those who promise to heed the message.

2. Age Assistance Advocacy Groups

I chose the title "Age Assistance," because even though they work on behalf of a broader spectrum of age groups, they certainly take into consideration the interests of retirees in the process. A compendium here would probably add 100 pages to the book, so I will give a few just as examples.

AAA

The American Automobile Association renders assistance to motorists and has a broad range of benefits for the traveler, including insurance. All ages are welcome to join. They can provide special assistance like obtaining an international driver's license for those goin abroad. Among other things they provide refresher driver courses for senior on line, defensive driver courses at their facilities, and give professional opinions on whether seniors should continue to drive if they are asked to do so. They claim their aim is to keep senior citizens driving as long as possible. AAA also provides what they term "viable transportation alternatives" for seniors.

American Legion

These are social organizations for military veterans of all kinds. The American Legion was chartered by Congress in 1919. In many cities that have posts, their building is a gathering place for those 50 years old and older including liquid libations and dancing. There are State Veterans Homes where the costs of living are usually shared between Medicaid, long term care insurance and private funds. "VA pays a modest share of the cost for each veteran living in a State Veterans Home."[2]

NRA

The National Rifle Association advocates for senior citizens in Washington, D.C. as needed and for them keeping their own firearms through a continuing feature article titled, "The Army Citizen," that culls cases of self-defense using firearms from the media and presents them to the public. All age groups are included, but senior citizens are certainly part of the story.[3]

VFW

The Veterans of Foreign Wars were established in 1899 to provide assistance to veterans. They are a major advocate for Veterans affairs in Washington. Here is their statement of advocacy direct from their website at vfw.org: "The VFW is one of the most respected voices in Washington, D.C., and within local governments across America. We advocate for justice for our nation's veterans, service members and military families on an array of issues and continue to be the voice for veterans everywhere. We regularly testify before Congress, meet with elected officials and rally our national network of VFW members and patriotic supporters to ensure our lawmakers put veterans first. When those who've served their country and those that support them stand together, we can not be ignored."[4]

The VFW does not just testify, but lobbies to shape future Veterans policies for male and female veterans. If you look on their website, you will discover what I call five pillars of support:

1. Lobbying Congress and the administration on veterans' needs and issues.

2. National Security & Foreign Affairs program working to identify threats and finding and proposing methods of dealing with them.

3. Women Veteran Advocacy to ensure the needs of women veterans are being met.

4. Grass Roots program "The VFW's Action Corps is the VFW's grassroots lobbying effort. Located in communities across the globe, this group work to inform and educate veterans and service members on the initiatives and policies that affect them and take the voice of veterans to local, state and national lawmakers."[4]

5. VA Health Care Watch monitors the Veterans Administration on their system and capabilities to "deliver veteran's feedback directly to VA officials in order to implement new programs and methods to ensure America's veterans receive the top quality care they deserve."[4]

The VFW is also a charitable organization giving youth scholarships. Looking back at their historical achievements shows their involvement on the national political stage: "Our voice was instrumental in establishing the Veterans

Administration, development of the national cemetery system, in the fight for compensation for Vietnam vets exposed to Agent Orange and for veterans diagnosed with Gulf War Syndrome. In 2008, we won a long-fought victory with the passing of a GI Bill for the 21st Century, giving expanded educational benefits to America's active duty service members, and members of the guard and reserves, fighting in Iraq and Afghanistan. We were the driving force behind the Veterans Access and Accountability Act of 2014, and continually fight for improved VA Medical Center services for women Veterans."[4]

"Besides helping fund the creation of the Vietnam, Korean War, World War II and Women in Military Service memorials, in 2005 the VFW became the first veterans' organization to contribute to building the new Disabled Veterans for Life Memorial, which opened in November 2010. And in 2015, we became the first supporter of the National Desert Storm War Memorial which is planned for construction at our nation's capital."[4]

3. Attend Town Hall Meetings

Political operatives who come to town often speak at what are termed, Town Hall Meetings. Usually there is a speaker running for office, trying to hold onto office, or seeking to inform the electorate at the local level as to policies on which they are working and then asking you for support.

Town Hall sessions are often give-and-take, or question and answer formats designed to allow us, the audience to get involved, let off steam, or at least get answers to questions that trouble us.

4. Attend/Organize Political Rallies/Demonstrations

Political rallies can be a lot of fun, especially if we can take spouses and children to listen to political speeches. This is a great way to show support for our favorite candidates and at the same time poses the possibility of having a picture taken with them. If one has aspirations of more direct future involvement, meeting the local political operatives can be both fun and rewarding, since they may come to recognize you and become friends in the process.

Demonstrations are a right of the people for free association. They are usually single issue oriented and provide an opportunity not only to meet and greet others of a similar political persuasion, but to achieve a feeling of a grass roots movement and solidarity of purpose.

One way of mobilizing support for an issue is done through rallies and demonstrations.

At the very least you may get to shout and relieve some tension. You also will come to feel a personal connection with the candidate and that becomes an even greater motivating factor in deciding to become more involved in the political process.

5. Blog or Article Writer

If you become a blog or article writer, you will discover there are classes you can take online to assist you in the process and train you for that medium. Writer's Digest has at least one class a month, or so it seems to be that frequent, on how to blog. After I complete this book, I plan to take the class myself. The cost may vary, but the likely cost is $99 with personal feedback on your work and direct advice on how to succeed at blogging. In case you did not know, there are tens of thousands of dollars one can make as an established blogger by acquiring advertisers who are in sympathy and step with your interests. These can be very lucrative with some making millions. That is why you see on social media tricks such as "If you answer these questions, you have an IQ of 145." The many tests that are on Facebook® do the same thing. Whoever puts those on gets you to at least see their ads. Clicks into their testing, results in more advertiser interest, since they count the number of clicks on a blog. I should know. I taught that in my International Marketing class for Travel University International in San Diego.

Articles can be moneymakers. Writing an article and selling may mean to your favorite magazines, or you can purchase a" Writers' Market" book providing a comprehensive list of publications seeking good writing. There has been an explosion of publications online and one can tap into such a market. The need for material is daily and massive. You may begin at $100 to $300 for an article, but the satisfaction of the first sale is euphoric and leads to more writing gigs that may be requested by them and other publishers.

6. Book Writer

I decided to take my own advice and write political books. This is one way to attempt to make a direct impact on the process nationally and it can be done from the comforts of home or even from a senior care facility! If you really want to vent your frustrations in a productive and meaningful way, this is an excellent course of action. Finding an agent can be frustrating itself, so you are forewarned. If you self publishes a book, you can send it to political operatives, give it as gifts to relatives at Christmas, give it to those opposed to your point of view and use it as a stepping stone to the other activities I have listed in these 25 activities.

Self publishing means you get to become a marketer as well, which can lead you to social media advertising, preparing a platform for sales such as a website or blog, and using advertising in papers and publications. I plan on sending this book to some key political people at author cost.

---

7. City Council Attendee

Attending City Council meetings is a way to stay informed of community activities, charities, and issues. Everything that goes on in a community should be of importance to all of us. There will be construction companies making proposals, Zoning Board actions that can have a strong effect on the community, calendars of events discussed, a civic problem brought up on everything from trash pickup and disposal to water quality, safety, and need for acquisition of water sources. This is also the way to become acquainted with local officials before and after meetings and taking a step to becoming a City Council Member. These days, meeting dates and subjects to be discussed appear on the city websites.

8. City Council Member/Mayor

If you want a direct voice in local government, becoming a City Council member certainly improves the prospect of having a direct vote in what happens in your community. This can also be viewed as another stepping stone up to the county level, or even to becoming mayor of the city, since you will have support of at least some of the other members in such an undertaking.

I thought about adding a separate item to my list of things with which to become involved, but being a mayor fits well in this category, since the mayor heads the City Council.

9. Club Member

There are clubs for every interest and many of them assist with meeting and greeting dignitaries of a political persuasion that love to speak to these groups to obtain support for their agendas and candidacies. This category encompasses everything from a garden club to a book club.

10. Correspondent to Congress and State Legislators

When I mention "correspondent," I mean writing letters and contacting members of Congress and the State Legislatures about political subjects near and dear to the heart. Some assistant is likely the recipient of your message and may be the gatekeeper in terms of getting your direct input to the representative. My daughter, Melanie, worked in Congressman Stenny Hoyer's office one summer which gave me a more direct input. Interns often are the ones used to aggregate yes's and no's on a particular piece of legislation and inform the representative of the wishes of their political base.

One may also send messages to the White House and the President. There are several people working as a conduit on political interest matters and on responding to the requests of constituents.

Some clubs, if they are politically savvy, will have a position of political correspondent to reach the appropriate levels of representation on issues that concern the club and report back to the club on results of their correspondence

11. County Hearing Attendance

County hearings are a lot like attending a City Council meeting. It is a place to meet and greet political operatives, as well as a way to stay informed on issues that may directly affect the community, especially on construction matters, road maintenance and other county activities. The floor is open to discuss issues in which you and your family or group may have a particular interest.

12. County Election Official

County leadership positions are mostly paid positions and one would have to put in an application to the County

Clerk, County Sheriff, County Attorney, County Appraiser, or County Tax Collector.

The position of Election Official is an important though temporary appointment and that is to oversee elections by sitting at a table, giving advice on voting procedures, handing out ballots, watching ballot boxes (if the county still uses paper ballots), and then counting the votes in an election. They work for the Supervisor of Elections for the County.

13. Host/Hostess for Meet the Candidate Neighborhood Parties

Anyone can be a host or hostess for a political candidate. Hors d' oeuvres and beverages of choice are all that you need for the party along with a commitment from the candidate to be present.

Personal story. When I lived in Fairfax Station, Virginia, I volunteered to work the phones for a political campaign for a candidate for the U.S. House of Representatives. The candidate was Bill Miller and he agreed to attend the house party. When he came for the party, we had canvassed the neighborhood and invited perhaps 50 couples to be present. We had the house in immaculate condition and served soft drinks and hors d'oeuvres as I suggested. He came to the party with tennis shoes on and said the reason for the tennis shoes was he was running hard for the office. The party was a success both for him and for our becoming better known in the community. In fact he received some excellent contributions that day.

14. Petition Starter, Marketer or Signer

There are two types of petitions:

1.) Petitions for Candidates. Candidates for political office must have a specified number of valid signatures. One can set outside a grocery store with permission, of course, and register customers going in and coming out. I found it is usually better to catch them going in, since they seem to be in a hurry to get home so the ice cream does not melt.

2.) Petitions for issues. Whatever the political issue and at whatever level you wish to petition for change or redress, on can get up a petition, again with valid signatures and present it alone, as a representative of an interest group, or with the group itself, or at least the leaders of the group.

15. Parade Participant or Watcher

Marching in a parade, having a business float, and perhaps getting together with others for a political party, candidate, or issue float with themes and decorations can be a fun thing for senior citizens to do. Then someone has to drive it, so why not volunteer for that duty, as well? Even being a watcher and cheering for the floats that are politically motivated, or booing them as the case may be can be both fun and rewarding. At least you can express yourself in public.

16. Political Campaign Volunteer

Every political campaign can use as many persons, as there are volunteers for support and assistance. There are never enough. Having worked in some of them I can tell you that at the very least "foot soldiers," that is what I call those willing to get on the phone for political support by voting and by soliciting donations, as well as distributing campaign brochures, signs, pins, and other paraphernalia are highly coveted.

The sincerest form of volunteering is donating and then getting friends and relatives to donate. Some candidates operate much like you may see local public television stations operating when they say at such and such a level you get one DVD or CD, but at the next two levels you get more. Hats, T-shirts, pens and pins are the staple "gifts" candidates give out. Bumper stickers are usually in a pile at their headquarters along with political support signs in the back room.

Do you have computer skills? They need you. Have you been an accountant? They need you track donations and spending. Are you an attorney? They could use your advice so as not to break any campaign laws. Can you walk? They need you to "pound the street" and knock on doors.

17. Precinct Committee Person

This is the real first grassroots organization in the political party chain leading all the way to the National Committee. The Precinct Committee Person operates at the direction and discretion of the Precinct Committee Chair. I just mentioned the "pound the street" and "knock on doors" people who are the first link in the voter chair by providing information, finding out about registration by asking questions, and delivering messages and trends to the Precinct Committee Chair.

18. Precinct Committee Chair

Depending on the part of the country, state and region where you are located and then on the various persons contact higher in the chain, The Precinct Committee Chair may be called Precinct Captain, Precinct Chairman, Precinct Chairwoman, or Precinct Committee Officer. They are elected to serve in that capacity by the American political party system.

They direct the activities by the other Precinct Committee members, collect information for those higher in the chain, and serve as a transmission belt going both up and down to the grassroots level. Smart Precinct Committee Chairs have their ears to the ground and report on dissatisfaction with the message of the candidates, issues they avoid or pound on too much and registration filters. Remember my story to begin the chapter. There are certain perks such as getting invited to inaugural balls at the state capitol.

19. Run for Political Office

The real problem with our political system today is the amount of money it takes to win an election, or at least put up a good fight. For a poorly opposed House of Representatives candidate in a district that has always been safe for one party, the total expenditures could still be as much as one million dollars. That includes offices in various cities for volunteers to staff, campaign costs of traveling around the territory by whatever means of transportation, marketing and advertising, merchandise, signs, posters, billboards and more.

If you decide to run, make sure to consult with the party at several levels, inform them of your background and issue orientation and solicit both funds and someone to run the campaign for you.

20. Sign Placer

If you already have some experience such as placing business signs for maximum exposure, then you are a valuable asset to a campaign. Knowing costs of placement, or better yet, where to place them for free, such as someone you know in the party that has an excellent piece of ground for placement adds considerable value to the campaign.

If you have a front yard, then you can place at least one sign in your yard for your candidate. Contact the campaign headquarters and find out how to get one. Perhaps you know neighbors who would either like, or at least not mind having one in their yard.

21. Social Media Master or Maven

Now I know there are millions of you who use social media on a daily basis. Some of our senior citizens I know are glued to it all daylong. Other of you come and go during the day. There is a chance someone who needs to see your "page" also needs to know your support for candidates, parties, or issues. I used the term "master" for the men and "maven" for the ladies. Maven may also be used for men, but in my experience, it is used more often for women.

Your comments on postings of others can have an effect, especially on the undecided. In the 2016 campaign I was pleased to see a number of my friends posted they voted already. During the campaign I provided information on where to find a ballot in advance and conduct absentee balloting to avoid the long lines that might be difficult for my senior friends to stand in line.

22. State Political Committee Member

I explained the process for being elected to the State Political Committee. In my case it was through a stroke of luck and having an advocate sitting in my class as a student. I should add that Jackie was a delegate to the National Convention. I did not know that at the time, but she was extremely well connected in Arizona political circles. I had no doubt that if I could have remained in Arizona and not enter the Army for my duty, I would have planned on eventually running at least for Governor.

Notice I mentioned national delegate. They are elected or selected from the national committees to attend the high-level political functions like conventions.

23. Volunteer Poll Watchers and Paid Election Officials

Various organizations solicit for poll workers and poll watchers besides the political party. Here is the online ad placed by the National Coalition on Black Civic Participation: "We need YOU to volunteer to become a pol worker or a poll monitor. Poll workers attend trainings with local election boards, identify problems and serve inside the polling place on Election Day. Poll watchers distribute voter education materials and serve as our eyes and ears on the ground. They submit incident reports to the Election Protection Hotline, 1-866-OUR VOTE, and to the National Coalition on Black Civic Participation's Election Day Command Center. Poll watchers work with voters and election officials to resolve problems before the polls close."[5]

Election officials are paid $145 on election day in Wisconsin and $300 in New York on Election Day. Election officials tend to come from the Precinct Committees, since they are "trusted" campaign members.

24. Voter Registration and Voting

Voter registration in the United States is required for voting in federal, state and local elections, except North Dakota, although the law allows cities to register voters for city elections.[8] Depending on the state registration takes place at the county and municipal level with cutoff dates normally prior to Election Day. A 2012 study showed 24% of eligible voters were not registered to vote for a number just over 50 million.[8]

Given the large numbers not voting, it is in the interests of both political parties to have voters interested in their views registered. Games are played here, such as getting together a voting drive that sounds like everyone is invited to vote, but where volunteers may go door to door in neighborhoods they think will be the most likely to support their political party. If they knock on the door and find someone unregistered a few simply question can be asked to determine their political orientation, then the volunteer decision can be to offer them a ride to the office to help get them registered, while not making the same offer to someone that might be against their party or views. This is where one can have a lot of fun and as I said, "play games," both with what one says and with what one does.

Of course, you can form your own mini-drive in a club, with relatives, or checking with friends.

Don't forget to vote yourself and if in your checking around someone of your beliefs and party needs a lift, then I recommend taking the. Calling them a day or two beforehand can be fun to get together with say five friends and then go to lunch afterwards at your treat. I say your treat, because it is a simple way to feel you accomplished something politically.

25. Wake up the Family

Waking up the family is not just on election day, but a lifelong effort to make sure family values are represented to children and grandchildren. Do not be afraid to talk politics with them and express your joy or anger at campaign issues and campaign results of having your candidate elected.

Your involvement in the political process can set a good example for everyone in the family. If you read the entire book, or if you are checking first at the end, my advice is for the Gray Zone to band together to generate Gray Power Politics to advance our issues and get the attention of the President and Congress. There are dozens of ways to become involved as I have enumerated to cause this to happen.

We are not without the numbers of voters needed to succeed. We are not without the will and capabilities to advance our objectives. We literally have political power that we can exercise in voting and acting as a unified pressure group. Furthermore, our political power grows daily as the population of the United States becomes even more numerous in the Gray Zone. Remember the projections all the way to 2060 are for us to increase in numbers. We are obligated to use that political power wisely to ensure the future for ourselves, our children, our grandchildren and the America we all want and deserve.

BIOGRAPHY LTC ROY E. PETERSON
U.S. Army Military Intelligence Retired

LTC Roy Peterson served as an Assistant Army Attaché in Moscow during the peak of the Cold War Years from 1983-1985, as the first U.S. Foreign Commercial Officer in the Russian Far East for the U.S. Department of Commerce with dual duty as a Visa Issuing Officer for the U.S. Department of State, and as the first IBM Regional Manager, Vladivostok, Russian Far East (1993-1995.

LTC Peterson is a recognized international trade and Russian political/military consultant. Roy was a recent faculty member with the University of Phoenix teaching global business, marketing, sales, management, military intelligence, unconventional warfare, and international trade.

Roy Peterson is a poet, songwriter, and award-winning bass voice singer.

Writing Credentials: LTC Peterson published 25 books, over 20 extensive secret intelligence studies, over 100 intelligence reports (unavailable), 2 MA theses, and 2 Institute publications.

Military Intelligence Credentials: Phoenix Advisor Vietnam; Commander, Military Intelligence Company, Germany; Manager, Army Security Clearances; 1st Army Staff Intelligence Advisor, Pentagon; Selected to replace Ollie North on Security Council; Presidential Representative to Russia On-Site Inspection Agency; Army Attaché, Moscow; 1st US Foreign Commercial Officer, Russian Far East; 1st IBM Manager Russian Far East; President Export Company; Honor Graduate, US Army Russian Institute; Russian language fluency; Human Intelligence Coordinator, 1st Gulf War. LTC

Peterson was awarded the Legion of Merit and Bronze Star among many decorations.

Academic Credentials: BA, Hardin-Simmons, MA University of Arizona, MA University of Southern California, MBA University of Phoenix, Ph.D., passed written and oral exams and remains ABD (all but done). Defense Language Institute, Russian. Honor Graduate US Army Russian Institute. Additional honors and awards provided upon request.

Business Credentials: President HPO International and TriCrown International, VP International Trade Company, VP Investment Company, VP Construction Development Company, VP Management Company. Sold trucks to Russia, 1st USDOC Foreign Commercial Officer in Russian Far East, 1st IBM Manager in Russian Far East, taught International Trade and Global Business. Management for University of Phoenix, Director New Business Development for ENSCO. Wrote operational and technical proposal for EG&G on Strategic Arms Limitation Talks Contract.

ENDNOTES

Chapter 1

1. Data Table: Data 360: http://data360.org/dsg.aspx?
Data_Set_Group_Id=195.

Chapter 2

1. "Alzheimer's Disease Fact Sheet." National Institute of
Health. nih.gov.

2. "Fact Sheet: Aging in the United States…" Population
Reference Bureau. www.prb.org/aging-united states-fact-
sheet. January 13, 2016.

3. "Drug Abuse Symptoms, Facts, and Statistics." Rehabs.com.
luxury.rehabs.com/ drug-abuse.

4. U.S. Census Bureau.

5. "How Many Seniors Really End Up in Nursing Homes?"
Nursing Home Diaries. nursinghomediaries.com /howmany.

6. "Nursing Homes." AARP. assets.aarp.org/ rgcenter /il/
fs10r_homes.pdf.

7. Found in "Myths and Stereotypes of Aging." Senor Living
Blog. Jeff Anderson. June 28. 2018. https://aplaceformom.
com/blog/14-18-4-aging-myths-dispelled/.

8. "7 Myths About Older People." Senior Planet.
https://seniorplanet.org/7-myths-about-old-people/
Accessed March 9, 2019.

9. "The FACTS." Statistical Abstract of the United States.

www.census.gov/compendia/statab.

10. "For the Best Sex of Your Life – Ask the Old People." Isabelle Kohn. <u>Harpers Bazaar</u>. October 27, 2018. **https://www.harpersbazaar.com/culture/features/a19607352/b est-sex-of-your-life-senior-sex-joan-price-interview/** Accessed March 9, 2019.

11. "Myths and Stereotypes of Aging." Senor Living Blog. Jeff Anderson. June 28. 2018. https://www.aplaceformom.com /blog/14-18-4-aging-myths-dispelled/.

12. Cavanaugh, J. C., & Blanchard-Fields, F. <u>Adult Development and Aging, (fifth edition)</u>. Belmont, CA: Wadsworth, Thomson Learning. 2006.

13. Bureau of Labor Statistics as quoted in note #11 above.

14. "Myths of Aging." <u>NPO Crossroads</u>. NPO. November 11, 2016.

15. Doyle, B. (1997, April 17). *Mythology*. Retrieved from <u>Encyclopedia Mythica</u>™: http://www.pantheon.org/articles/ m/mythology.html Explanation in <u>NPO</u> as listed in note #14.

16. Sather, J. (2008, January 28). *Retire these 10 myths of aging*. Retrieved from Healthline (licensed from StayWell): http://www.healthline.com/sw/wl-retire-these-10-myths-of-aging as cited and quoted in <u>NPO</u> note #14.

17. "Top 2 Myths about Self-Defense for NRA Family. The National Rifle Association. Wendy LaFever, April 14, 2018. https://www.nrafamily.org/articles/2018/4/14/top-2-myths-about-self-defense-for-seniors/.

18. Rowe, J. W., & Kahn, R. L. (2009). *Breaking down the myths of aging: Successful aging* Retrieved from eNotalone: You are not alone. Articles and forums about relationships and personal growth: http://www.enotalone.com/article/4586.html. As quoted in NPO. See note #14.

19. Birren, J. (2002). Gerontology. In <u>Encyclopedia of public health</u> (Gerontology, the study of aging). Retrieved from encyclopedia.com: http://www.encyclopedia.com/doc/1G2-3404000376.html.

<u>Chapter 3</u>

1. "Brainy Quotes," Brainy Quote. www.brainyquote.com/topics/government.

2. U.S. Census Bureau. <u>Quick Facts</u>: https://www.census.gov/ quickfacts/fact/ table/ US/PST045217).

3. <u>The Washington Post,</u> "What Does a $15 Minimum Wage do to the Economy?" Mark Ingraham. January 11, 2019. (Wonkblog).

4. <u>Ibid.</u>

6. U.S. Department of Justice Chart 2015.

7. Texas.

8. National Council on Aging. https://www.ncoa.org/economic-security/money-management/scams-security/top-10-scams-targeting-seniors/ (Accessed Feb 10, 2019. No date on the document.).

9. "Danger in Drugs from Canada," The Washington Times. Peter J. Pitts. August 10, 2016.

10. The Secret Language of Money, Daniel Krueger. The McGraw Hill Companies, 2009.

11. Facebook Help Center | Facebook. https://www.facebook.com/help/901370616673951**11**. What Your Nonprofit Needs to Know About Facebook's New Fundraising Tools. Nonprofit Tech for Good, July 10, 2016.

12. William Webster, ex-FBI and CIA director, helps feds nab Jamaican phone scammer. The Washington Post. Tom Jackman. February 12, 2019. https://www.fairus.org/issue/publications-resources/fiscal-burden-illegal-immigration-united-states-taxpayers.

Chapter 4

1. Social Security Administration Historical Research Note #2 "The History and Development of the Lump Sum Death Benefit," Larry DeWitt, 1996 and updated to 2006.

2. Burial Allowance. Military.com.

3. "What is the Average Cost of Cremation," US Funerals Online. Sara J. Marsden, Editor in Chief. July 7, 2018.]

4. "Taxation of Social Security Benefits." Social Security Administration Historical Research Note #12. Social Security Administration. Larry DeWitt. February 2001.

5. Footnote 5: "Is Social Security Taxable," by Dan Caplinger. The Motley Fool Website. September 29, 2018.

6. "Here's the Average Social Security Benefit for 2019" Maurie Backman. <u>The Motley Fool Website</u>. October 16, 2018.

7. "Social Security Benefits: Will They Be There…" <u>Nolo.com</u> www.nolo.com/legal-encyclopedia/social-security-benefits-retirement-32416.html.

8. "Social Security Act Amendments of 1950. H.R. 6000, August 28, 1950. Public Law 81-734." Social Security Administration.

9. "How Much Does Assisted Living and Home Care Cost in the US?" <u>Senior Living.org</u> (accessed February 21, 2019).

10. "Long-Term Budget Outlook Has Improved Considerably Since 2010, but Remains Challenging." Richard Kogan, Paul N. Van de Water, and Yixuan Huang. November 15, 2018. <u>Center on Budget Policies and Priorities</u>.

11. "Maternal and Child Health and Mental Retardation Planning Amendments of 1963." <u>Social Security Administration.</u> H.R. 7544, October 24, 1963, Public Law 88-156, Title XVII.

12. "A Major Change is Coming to Social Security in 2022." Sean Williams. May 14, 2018. The Motley Fool.

13. "Series of Morbidity Reports." <u>Centers for Disease Control and Prevention</u>.

14. "Analysis of the 2018 Social Security Trustees Report." <u>Highlights of the 2018 Annual Report: Social Security Policy Papers</u>. National Committee to Preserve Social Security and Medicare. June 6, 2018.

15. <u>LegalBeagle</u>. https://legalbeagle.com/5340774-penalties-social-security-fraud.html.

16. "News Today." <u>National Right to Life</u> January 18, 2018.

17. "Abortion Rate, Abortions Overall Down in U.S." CDC. thedialog.org/featured/abortion-rate-abortions-overall...s-cdc-reports. November 27, 2018.

18. "Social Security Expansion Bill Poised to Gain Traction in Congress." CNBC. Sarah O'Brien. February 24, 2019. http://www.msn.com/en-us/money/retirement/social-security-expansion-bill-poised-to-gain-traction-in-congress/ar-BBTYWqh?li=BBnb7Kz&ocid=iehp.

19. Government Tracking of Bills. https://www.govtrack.us/congress/bills/subjects/social_security/4833.

Chapter 5

1. When illness is imaginary, its entirely a different case...articles.latimes.com/2003/han/20/health/he-hypochondria20.

2. Source: Gallup Survey 1999 and National Pain Foundation Telephone Poll, 2002.

3. Americans Prefer Drug-Free Pain Management Over Opioids (2017). https://news.galljup.com/reports/21676.

4. "National Pain Foundation Report." National Pain Foundation. http://nationalpainreport.com/ national-pain-foundation.

5. "U.S. Retail Sales of Homeopathic Medicine by Type 2018." <u>Statista</u>. https://www.statista.com/statistics/466508/us-retail-sales-of-homeopathic-and-herbal-remedies/. Accessed February 24, 2019.

6. "Does Epsom Salt Work? The Science of Epsom Salt Bathing for Recovery from Muscle Pain, Soreness, or Injury." PainScience.com Paul Ingraham. Updated January 19, 2019.

7. "Liniment." <u>Science Direct</u>. Dr. Galer. (Taken from the book <u>Pain Medication Secrets</u> (third edition). 2013. https://www.sciencedirect.com/topics/medicine-and-dentistry/liniment.

8. "Opioid (Narcotic) Pain Medications." <u>WebMD</u>.

9. "Opioids." National Institute on Drug Abuse. https://www.drugabuse.gov/drugs-abuse/opioids# summary-of-the-issue. Accessed February 25, 2019.

10. Opioids.gov.

11. "Tetrahydrocannabidiol." <u>Wikipedia</u>. https://en. wikipedia.org/wiki/ Tetrahydrocannabinol, Accessed February 25, 2019.

12. "U.S. approves first prescription drug made from marijuana." <u>The Denver Post</u>. June 25, 2018.

13. "CBD in Marijuana may Worsen Glaucoma. Raise Eye Pressure." <u>Science News</u>. December 14, 2018. Source reported from Indiana University.

14. "Letter from the Director." Nora D. Volkow, M.D. Director. <u>National Institute on Drug Abuse.</u> Updated June 2018.

15. 10 Things Seniors should know about Medical Marijuana. <u>Senior Directory</u>. Accessed February 24, 2019. https://seniordirectory.com/articles/info/10-things-seniors-should-know-about-medical-marijuana.

16. "11/14: Alzheimer's Most Feared Disease – <u>Marist Poll</u>. marist**poll**.marist.edu/1114-alzheimers-most-feared-disease. November 15, 2012.

17. "Alzheimer's Disease Fact Sheet." <u>National Institute on Aging</u>. Reviewed August 17, 2017.

18. "Chemical in California Shrub Could Help Treat Alzhemier's Disease. In nextbigfuture. Brian Wang, February 21, 2019. https://www.nextbigfuture.com/2019/02/chemical-in-california-shrub-could-help-treat-alzheimers-disease.html#more-154069.

19. "Long-term Care Costs Continue to Rise." <u>Modern Healthcare</u>, from The Associated Press, May 10, 2016.

20. <u>IRS Questions</u>. https://www.irs.gov/faqs/itemized-deductions-standard-deduction/medical-nursing-home-special-care-expenses/medical-nursing-home-special-care-expenses.

21. For a great description of physical and mental abuse read my three Life Stories covered in the "Where the Horny Toads Play" trilogy. The three volumes are "Where the Horny Toads Play," When Sunsets Glow" and "On the Edge of Night." Roy E. Peterson, TriCrownbooks.

22. "Fact Checking Trump on Veterans Affairs." Interview of Quil Lawrence by Robert Siegel, Host of <u>All Things Considered</u>. August 23, 2017.

23. "Homeless Health Concerns: Medline Plus." Last updated January 29, 2019. medlineplus.gov.

24. "How High Drug Prices and Big Lobbying Budgets Go Together for Big Pharma" <u>Forbes</u>. By JAY HANCOCK AND ELIZABETH LUCAS April 26, 2018 Accessed February 26 2019. http://fortune.com/2018/04/26/drug-prices-diabetes-lobbying/

25. <u>Wikipedia</u>
https://en.wikipedia.org/wiki/Cost_of_drug_development

26. Herper, Matthew (11 August 2013). "The Cost Of Creating A New Drug Now $5 Billion, Pushing Big Pharma To Change". <u>Forbes,</u> Pharma & Healthcare. Retrieved 17 July 2016. As reported in <u>Wikipedia</u>
https://en.wikipedia.org/wiki/Cost_of_drug_development.

27. Gaffney, Alexander. <u>"FDA Publishes All User Fee Rates for Fiscal Year 2014 | RAPS"</u>. www.raps.org. from <u>Wikipedia</u>
https://en.wikipedia.org/wiki/Cost_of_drug_development.

28. Herper, Matthew. "The Truly Staggering Cost Of Inventing New Drugs". <u>Forbes</u>. from <u>Wikipedia</u>
https://en.wikipedia.org/wiki/Cost_of_drug_development.

29. "Trump Proposes to Lower Drug Prices by Basing Them on Other Countries' Costs." Robert Pear. <u>New York Times</u>. October 25, 2018.

30. <u>Chicago Tribune</u>. "The Same Pill that Sells for $1,000 in the U.S. Sells for $4 in India." Ketake Gokhale. January 4, 2016.

31. "Hepatitis C Drugs in 2019: Price Drops and Generic Pipeline in Place." Stephen Holt, MD.

<u>Chapter 6</u>

1. "Reports: Illegal immigrants receiving Medicaid costs taxpayers $18.5 billion annually By Bethany Blankley. <u>Watchdog.org</u> Oct 19, 2018.

2. Cato Institute.

3. Illegal Immigration Costs U.S. taxpayers $155 Billion per year (State and Federal). <u>Natural News</u>. Lance D. Johnson. Devember 2018. Note the number came from the Federation for American Immigration Reform (FAIR).

4. "Even Cato Agrees: A Border Wall Can Pay for Itself." <u>FAIR.</u> Steven A, Camarota. May 1, 2017. https://cis.org/Camarota/Even-Cato-Agrees-Border-Wall-Can-Pay-Itself. Accessed February 27, 2019.

5. Cato Flubs Illegal Immigrant Numbers When Criticizing President Trump. Newsandtimes.com. https://www.newsandtimes.com/politics/2017/07/. **July 2017.**

6. "New Research: The impact of illegal aliens on crime rates, data codebook and 'do file.'" The Crime Prevention Research Center. January 17, 2018.

7. "Criminal Alien Statistics." GAO-11-187, Government Accountability Office. March 2011.

8. "Criminal Alien Statistics." GAO-18-433, Government Accountability Office. Published July 17, 2018. Publicly Released August 16, 2018.

9. "Southeastern Provision Owner James Brantley Pleads Guilty to Federal Information." <u>Press Release</u>. The United States Attorney's Office, Eastern District of Tennessee. September 12, 2018.

10. <u>NBC News Report</u>. February 19, 2019.

11. "The Dark Side of Illegal Immigration: Fats, Figures and Statistics on Illegal Immigration." http://www.usillegalaliens.com/impacts_of_illegal_immigration_Diseases. html.

12. "Six Diseases Return To US as Migration Advocates Celebrate 'World Refugee Day'" Breitbart. June 19, 2016. <u>https://www.breitbart.com/politics/2016/06/19/diseases-thought-eradicated-world-refugee-day/</u>.

13. "Crisis of Seriously Ill Migrants Slams Border Patrol — TB, Pneumonia, Influenza, Parasites." <u>Judicial Watch Blog. Corruption Chronicles.</u> January 7, 2019. Found on Social Media.

14. "Report: Welfare Use by Immigrant Households with Children. A Look at Cash, Medicaid, Housing, and Food Programs." Steven A. Camarota. Center for Immigration Studies. April 5. 2011.

15 . "How American Citizens Finance $18.5 Billion in Healthcare for Unauthorized Immigrants." Chris Conover. <u>Forbes.</u> February 26, 2016. Accessed February 28, 2019. https://www.forbes.com/sites/theapothecary/2018/02/26/

how-american-citizens-finance-health-care-for-undocumented-immigrants/#6361770b12c4.

16. "Remittances Play Huge Roll in Immigrant Economy." <u>The Hill</u>. Rafael Bernal and Mike Lillis. October 31, 2016.

17. "Remittances: Illegal Immigration's Hidden Tax." <u>American Greatness</u>. Spencer P. Morrison. June 20, 2018.

18. "Remittances from Abroad are Major Economic Assets for Some Developing Countries." <u>Pew Research Center</u>, Drew Desilver. January 29, 2018. http://www.pewresearch.org/fact-tank/2018/01/29/remittances-from-abroad-are-major-economic-assets-for-some-developing-countries/.

19. "Migration and Remittances: Recent Developments and Outlook" <u>Migration and Development Brief 30</u>. World Bank. December 2018.

20. "Migrants' Remittances to Mexico, Central America Jump to $53 Billion in 2018." <u>Breitbart</u>. January 2, 2019.

<u>Chapter 7</u>

Note: I did not use endnotes for the quotes in the Chapter, since I cited them in the text.

1. 2nd Amendment, <u>U.S. Constitution.</u>

2. U.S. Crime Rates by County, 2014. <u>Washington Post.</u> Check graphic on Internet.

3. "Electoral Map Presidential Election 2016." <u>Internet Graphic</u>.

4. "Crime in the United States 2012, 2012 Crime Clock Statistics." <u>Uniform Crime Report</u>. FBI, 2012.

5. <u>FBI Crime Statistics, Uniform Crime Report</u> https://ucr.fbi.gov/crime-in-the-u.s.

6. <u>USA LifeExpectancy</u>. https://www.worldlifeexpectancy. com/usa-cause-of-death-by-age-and-gender.

7. <u>National Center for Health Studies</u>. https://www.cdc.gov/nchs/fastats/leading-causes-of-death.htm 2016.

8. <u>Medical News Today</u>. https://www.medicalnewstoday.com/articles/282929.php Accessed March 5, 2019.

9. "How Gun Policies Affect Mass Shootings." <u>RAND Corporation.</u> Accessed March 5, 2019. https://www.rand.org/research/gun-policy/analysis/mass-shootings.html

10. <u>Internet Graphic Quote</u> by John F. Kennedy.

11. <u>Internet Graphic Quote</u> by Joseph Story.

12. FactCheck.org. Misquoting Yamamoto. <u>THE WIRE</u> *By Brooks Jackson*. *Posted on May 11, 2009. https://www.factcheck.org /2009/05/misquoting-yamamomo/*

<u>Chapter 8</u>

1. <u>Pet Food Politics: The Chihuahua in the Coal Mine</u>. Marion Nestle. University of California Press, 2008.

2. <u>Encyclopedia Britannica</u>. "The Jungle." Novel by Upton Sinclair, written by Kate Lohnes, Last Updated March 4, 2019.

---

3. <u>Cornucopia</u>. "USDA Sued for Removing Country-of-Origin Labeling on Meat. (Cattle Ranchers Sue to Return Country-of-Origin Labeling as found in <u>U.S. News & World Report</u> by Nicholas K. Geranios, Associated Press, June 21, 217.)

4. <u>Country-of-Origin Labeling for Foods and the WTO Trade Dispute on Meat Labeling</u>. Joel L. Green, Analyst in Agricultural. Congressional Research Service. December 5, 2015. https://fas.org/sgp/crs/misc/RS22955.pdf.

5. "U.S. Approves Purchase of Smithfield." <u>Politico</u>. Douglas Palmer. September 6, 2013.

6. "Organic Vs. Free-range Chicken." <u>SFGate</u>. <u>https://homeguides.sfgate.com/organic-vs-freerange-chicken-79168.html</u>.

7. "Another Side of Tilapia," <u>The New York Times</u>. Elisabeth Rosenthal, May 2, 2011.

8. MedlinePlus. <u>https://medlineplus.gov/foodlabeling.html accessed March 7</u>, 2019.

9. "From almond milk to veggie burgers, does anyone really have trouble knowing what these products are?" Shoshana Weissmann and Jessica Almy, Opinion, USA Today contributors Published 6:00 a.m. ET March 2, 2019 | Updated 12:04 p.m. ET March 2, 2019.

<u>Chapter 9</u>

1. "Advocacy Groups. <u>The Senior List</u>, Amie Clark. Blog: theseniorlist.com

2. "State Veterans Home." <u>The American Legion</u>. Accessed on March 9, 2019. https://www.legion.org/ veteranshealthcare/ state/homes.

3. NRA. <u>nra.org.</u>

4. Veterans of Foreign Wars. vfw.org.

5. National Coalition on Black Civic Participation webpage.

https://www.ncbcp.org/volunteer_to_become_a_poll_watch er_poll_worker/

6. National Coalition on Black Civic Participation webpage. https://www.ncbcp.org/volunteer_to_become_a_poll_watch er_poll_worker/.

7. "Voter Registration in the United States." <u>Wikipedia</u>. Wikipedia.org. Accessed March 10, 2019.

8. "Voter Registration." <u>Wikipedia</u>. En.wikipedia.org/wiki/ Voter registration.